The Sinn Féin Rebellion
as They Saw It

Burnt-out shell of General Post Office, showing the fallen flagstaff which bore the Republican Flag

THE SINN FEIN REBELLION AS THEY SAW IT

MARY LOUISA and
ARTHUR HAMILTON NORWAY

Edited and with an Introduction by
KEITH JEFFERY

IRISH ACADEMIC PRESS
DUBLIN • PORTLAND, OR

Sinn Fein Rebellion as They Saw It
Incorporating
The Sinn Fein Rebellion as I Saw It
First published in 1916 by Smith, Elder & Co., London
Reprinted in 1999 (incorporating Irish Experiences in War
[first publication]) by
IRISH ACADEMIC PRESS
44, Northumberland Road, Dublin 4, Ireland,
and in the United States of America by
IRISH ACADEMIC PRESS
c/o ISBS, 5804 NE Hassalo Street, Portland, OR 97213

Website: www.iap.ie

© Irish Academic Press 1999

Introduction © Keith Jeffery 1999

British Library Cataloguing in Publication Data
Norway, Mrs
 The Sinn Fein rebellion as I saw it
 1. Norway, Mrs – Correspondence 2. Ireland – History – Easter
 Rising, 1916 3. Ireland – History, Military – 20th century
 4. Ireland – History – Easter Rising, 1916 – Personal
 narratives
 I. Title II. Norway, Arthur Hamilton
 941.5'0821
 ISBN 0 7165 2664 6

Library of Congress Cataloging-in-Publication Data
Norway, Hamilton, Mrs., d. 1932.
 [Sinn Fein Rebellion as I saw it]
 The Sinn Fein Rebellion as they saw it / by Mary Louisa and Arthur
 Hamilton Norway; edited and with an introduction by Keith Jeffery.
   p. cm.
 Includes The Sinn Fein Rebellion as I saw it, by Mrs. Hamilton
 Norway and Arthur Hamilton Norway's Irish experiences in war.
 Sinn Fein Rebellion as I saw it originally published: London:
 Smith, Elder, 1916.
 Text of A.H. Norway's memoir, Irish experiences in war, is taken
 from a photocopy in the papers of Dr. Leon Ó Broin in the National
 Library of Ireland (MS 24,894).
 Includes bibliographical references.
 ISBN 0-7165-2664-6
 1. Ireland–History–Easter Rising, 1916– Personal narratives.
 2. Norway, Arthur H. (Arthur Hamilton), 1859–1938. 3. Norway.
 Hamilton, Mrs., d. 1932. I. Jeffrey, Keith. II. Norway, Arthur H.
 (Arthur Hamilton), 1859–1938. Irish experiences in war.
 III. Title. IV. Title: Irish experiences in war.
 DA965.N67A3   1999
 941.5082'1–DC21   98–53977
                                                         CIP

Printed by Creative Print and Design (Wales), Ebbw Vale

Contents

List of Illustrations

Sketch Maps

Acknowledgements

I would particularly like to acknowledge the help and encouragement I have received from the Hamilton Norways' granddaughters, Shirley Norway and Heather Mayfield. Alan Bairner, Lindsay Duguid, Noel Kissane, Eunan O'Halpin, Christopher Shorley, Jacquey Visick and the staff of the Australian Dictionary of Biography assisted during the writing of the Introduction, much of which was drafted while I was a Visiting Fellow at the Australian National University and the Australian Defence Force Academy. At both places I found much congenial and stimulating academic company. Financial support for my stay in Australia was provided by the British Council, the British Academy, the Australian Defence Force Academy and my own institution, the University of Ulster, to all of which I am most grateful.

Note Regarding the Editing
of the Texts

This volume contains *The Sinn Fein Rebellion as I Saw It*, by Mrs Hamilton Norway, originally published by Smith, Elder & Co. of London in 1916, and 'Irish Experiences in War' by Mrs Norway's husband, Arthur Hamilton Norway, which is being published here for the first time. The text of *The Sinn Fein Rebellion as I Saw It* is reproduced exactly as first published. Arthur Hamilton Norway's memoir, 'Irish Experiences in War', is taken from a photocopy in the papers of Dr Leon Ó Broin in the National Library of Ireland (MS 24,894). The document consists of twenty-nine typescript pages with some holograph amendments, none of which materially affect the sense of the writing. I have, therefore, provided only the final wording given by the author. The text may be incomplete. It ends abruptly at the end of a page, although with a complete sentence. Attempts to locate the original have failed and it now appears to be lost. A very few obvious misspellings (such as 'Harding' for 'Hardinge') have been corrected, but the punctuation and capitalisation of the original has been retained. So as not to interfere unduly with the flow of the narrative, I have made only the very minimum of annotations, and have not, for example, provided biographical details of well-known Irish personages or others sufficiently identified in the text.

Introduction

Mrs Hamilton Norway is historically rather an elusive figure. Apart from *The Sinn Fein Rebellion as I Saw It* she has left few public traces of her seventy-one-year life. Even the brief mention of her death in *The Times* has virtually disappeared. According to the *Official Index to The Times* her passing was noted in the first and second editions of the newspaper on 25 June 1932.[1] But only the final edition of the paper has generally been preserved (for example in microfilm copies) and not even *The Times* cuttings department has kept a copy of her death-notice.[2] Other than her memoir of the 1916 Rising she only survives through her family relationships: in particular her husband, Arthur Hamilton Norway (1859–1938), who was Secretary to the Irish General Post Office from 1912 to 1916, and her son, Nevil Shute Norway (1899–1960), who, writing as 'Nevil Shute', became an immensely successful author of popular fiction.

Mary Louisa Norway came from a family of British imperial soldiers and civil servants. Her father, Frederick Gadsden, was a major-general in the Indian Army. Beginning in the Indian Police, her brother Edward ended up as Inspector-General of Prisons in Madras.[3] Mary was raised 'very well up in all the usages of polite society; ... there was little', recalled her son, 'that she did not know about precedence, visiting cards, calling and "at home" days.'⁴ In 1891 she married Arthur Hamilton Norway, a junior official in the General Post Office with literary talent and ambitions. In 1887 *The Government Official. A Novel* was published, written by C. E. L. Riddell, 'with the assistance of A. H. Norway'.⁵ During the 1890s he wrote 'two charming additions to the "Highways and Byways Series"',⁶ *Devon and Cornwall* (1897) and *Yorkshire* (1899), as well as a *History of the Post-Office Packet Service* (1895) in which he drew on his own Cornish family background. Later on he added a novel *(Parson Peter, A Tale of the Dart)*, a travel book *(Naples Past and Present)* and a study of Dante's *Divine Comedy*.⁷ He also wrote a substantial memoir of his own time in Ireland – 'Irish Experiences in War' – supplementing his wife's account and which is here published for the first time. Writing ran in the family. Norway's mother, Georgina, was a prolific author, mostly of children's books, for example the *Adventures of Johnnie Pascoe* (1889) and *Little Marjorie's Secret* (1898).⁸ It is therefore not surprising perhaps that the Norways' younger son, Nevil, should have taken up writing as a career.

Arthur Hamilton Norway was a well-regarded and successful civil servant. In 1907 he became an assistant secretary and head of the Post Office staff branch. Here he was central in the implementation of the reforms which Herbert Samuel introduced after he became Postmaster-General in 1910. These included 'the abolition of the old and bad system of "blind alley" employment for boy messengers', whereby four thousand of the fourteen thousand messengers were dismissed each year when they reached the age of sixteen.⁹ After his death a former colleague wrote of him as 'a man of high character and lofty ideals … combined with a generous and kindly nature, which endeared him to all his colleagues. During his period of staff administration he won the respect of the post office staff generally by his combination of justice with kindheartedness'.¹⁰

Norway suffered progressively from deafness, which his son reckoned kept him from rising to the highest levels of the public service. Indeed he viewed his father's appointment in September 1912 to head the post office in Ireland as not so much a promotion – for he remained at the assistant secretary grade – as 'being shunted into a dead end' in view of his increasing disability.[11] In his own memoir Norway adduced personal reasons concerning the health of his wife and elder son, Fred, as persuading him to move to Ireland. But there was also a political dimension to the Irish appointment. Following the amalgamation of the Irish and British post offices in 1831 (apparently because of 'defects in the working of the Irish post office'[12]), the secretaryship to the Irish department had generally been filled by 'one of the higher officials' from the London headquarters in St Martin's-le-Grand.[13] Norway's appointment clearly fitted into this pattern, but when considering who should succeed Sir Reginald Egerton, an Englishman who had headed the Irish post office since 1898, Herbert Samuel can hardly have been ignorant of the political ramifications which accompanied appointment to the higher ranks of the civil service in Ireland. It is possible that Samuel had no opportunity for much 'quiet, calm deliberation' about this matter of departmental staffing. At precisely the period when the Dublin job was being settled, Samuel himself was embroiled in defending his public reputation during the 'Marconi scandal', when accusations were made of improper share dealing on his part and that of his ministerial colleagues Lloyd George and Rufus Isaacs.[14] Yet Norway can be seen as suited for the Irish job. He was clearly well-qualified, and could be regarded as a 'safe pair of hands' for a potentially difficult position. He was, moreover, 'inclined' to the 'case for Home Rule'.[15] In addition, with his growing deafness (as his son afterwards suspected), he might not have nursed long-term ambitions to stay in Dublin, or even with the civil service. In short, he was able, available, politically sympathetic and probably amenable to the opportunity of early retirement.

When Norway was being appointed Ireland was apparently well on the road to Home Rule. In April the third Government of Ireland Bill had been introduced into parliament. The proposed legislation provided for an Irish parliament and executive to take control of all domestic business, while matters such as defence and foreign affairs would remain in the hands of the United Kingdom parliament in London. It was widely assumed (not least among Ulster unionists) that John Redmond, the leader of the Irish parliamentary party, would in due course become the first prime minister of Ireland. With this in mind, and also continuing a policy adopted by its Conservative and Unionist predecessor, Asquith's Liberal government had taken to appointing increasing numbers of Catholic Irish nationalists to government positions.[16]

Although under the proposed Home Rule legislation postal services were excluded from the competence of an Irish parliament, Norway's appointment, over the head of an Irish assistant secretary with strong nationalist sympathies, James MacMahon, was widely criticised by nationalists. Some local authorities passed resolutions condemning the appointment of an Englishman who, it was noted, was both a Protestant and a Mason. *The Leader,* a Dublin weekly edited by D. P. Moran which vigorously championed Irish-Ireland ideas, asserted that the affair made a mockery of Home Rule and was a conspiracy fomented by 'the Jew financier' Samuel and 'the intellectual coon' Augustine Birrell (Chief Secretary for Ireland since 1907).[17] The *Sinn Féin Weekly* described the appointment as 'one of the grossest jobs yet perpetrated' and 'an insult to every Irishman in the Post Office'.[18] Nationalist representatives lobbied to change Samuel's decision. The prominent M.P. Tim Healy wrote to his brother that there was 'great searching of hearts because of the threatened appointment of a Mr. Norway, from London, to succeed Egerton, a Catholic, as secretary to the Post Office. All the bishops, including Dr. O'Donnell, wrote in vain to Redmond and Dillon. Herbert Samuel saw Redmond several times. 'The action of the Government', he concluded, 'shows that they have no belief that Home Rule will become law.'[19] The question of Norway's position came up again early in 1915 when the Nationalist M.P. John Dillon raised it with Samuel's successor as Postmaster-General, Charles Hobhouse. Dillon asserted that Samuel had agreed to appoint Norway for only two years, after which he would be replaced by an Irishman. Hobhouse, who had also been lobbied by John Redmond and the Belfast Nationalist M.P., Joseph Devlin, denied that any such promise had been made, but he conceded that Norway would only keep his present position until the Home Rule government came in when he would be 'abolished': 'that may be a year hence or two years or three years. We do not want him back in the G.P.O.', he added, 'and he will not be sorry to obtain abolition terms.'[20]

Norway was not unaware of the sensitivities accompanying his public position in Dublin. When Sir Matthew Nathan, his former superior at the Post Office in London, was appointed permanent under-secretary to the Irish Office in August 1914, Norway advised him not to join the Kildare Street Club as 'in the minds of Nationalists it is identified irreparably with a narrow and rather bitter type of Unionism which they resent'. Norway himself had joined the Sackville Street Club, which although a Protestant establishment was less closely identified with political unionism. Evidently drawing on his own experience, he stressed that strongly-held nationalist feelings existed 'to an extent which is worth attention from an Englishman taking up duty here for the first time and hoping, as I presume you do, to occupy a position of friendly relations with both sides'.[21] Such evidence as there is suggests that Norway lived up to this admirable standard. Tim Healy recalled long afterwards that Norway had 'behaved in Dublin most impartially'.[22] He also supervised great improvements in the G.P.O. headquarters in Dublin. As his wife noted, when he

17

arrived in Ireland the public office was a 'miserable, dirty little place', and Norway saw to it that plans were implemented to reconstruct the building, providing a grand new hall with an entrance under the central portico, as it remains to this day, albeit once again rebuilt following the events of Easter 1916.

When they first moved to Ireland, the Norways leased an agreeable 'rambling country house' called South Hill at 91 Mount Merrion Avenue in the south Dublin suburb of Blackrock. For their two sons, Fred and Nevil, accustomed to life in the more urban London district of Ealing, the house 'opened up new country pleasures we had hardly dreamed of'.[23] When war broke out in August 1914, Fred was living at home and studying at Trinity College, Dublin, while his fifteen-year-old brother was a pupil at Shrewsbury School in England. Fred quickly secured a commission in the Duke of Cornwall's Light Infantry and soon after Easter 1915 was drafted to the Western Front where in June he was seriously wounded by German shell-fire and died after three weeks in hospital.[24] He was still only nineteen years old. The following autumn, his father gave up the lease of South Hill and the family moved into the Royal Hibernian Hotel in Dawson Street. Nevil speculated not only that the increasing cost of maintaining South Hill was a worry for his father, but also that 'the house held so many memories of Fred for my mother and myself that it would be better to get rid of it and start again'.[25] So it was that Mrs Hamilton Norway witnessed the 1916 Rising from the enviably central location of one of Dublin's leading hotels.

The Sinn Fein Rebellion as I Saw It contains a set of four letters which Mrs Norway wrote for family consumption beginning on Easter Tuesday, 25 April, the second day of the Rising. Although the final letter was not completed until 26 May, the bulk of the account was written during the Rising itself and constitutes an especially vivid narrative of the Easter week events. 'For these letters', she wrote, 'I claim no literary merit: they were written during a period of extraordinary strain for family perusal only, and are a faithful record hour by hour of the Sinn Fein rebellion as I saw it.'[26] The text usefully complements other existing contemporary eyewitness accounts written by south Dublin residents, perhaps most importantly that of the writer James Stephens, sympathetic to the Sinn Féin cause,[27] but also the letters of Alfred Fannin, a comfortably-off Protestant businessman.[28] Mrs Norway's perspective combined that of the administration, which she experienced through her husband, and of a comparatively detached middle-class English observer. The reviewer for the *Times Literary Supplement,* indeed, extravagantly concluded that Mrs Norway was 'not one of the Unionist "wreckers" who are said to view the recent rebellion with no sense of proportion, but – judging by her remarks about Sir E. Carson and the Ulster Volunteers – a radical Home Ruler'.[29] Arthur Hamilton Norway's candid and shrewdly-observed memoir further amplifies the story from an official 'Dublin Castle' perspective.

At times the various accounts overlap. Every commentator reported rumours. On the second day of the Rising Stephens wrote that 'the rumours began, and I think it will be many a year before the rumours cease'.[30] Some of these turned out to be completely false – for example the wild tales reported by Mrs Norway early in the week of widespread insurrection outside Dublin, or that Sir Roger Casement had been shot in London. Some of these, including one that Jacob, the biscuit manufacturer whose factory was occupied by rebels, had declared that he would 'never make another biscuit in Ireland', she corrected in footnotes. Other tales reflected a perhaps understandable misinterpretation of events. Writing on the afternoon of Friday 28 April, Mrs Norway recorded that on Wednesday 'three of the ringleaders' had been caught, 'and it is said they were shot immediately!' This story clearly stemmed from the murder at about 10.15 on Wednesday morning of Francis Sheehy Skeffington and two journalists on

the orders of a deranged British army officer and fellow-
Irishman, Captain J. C. Bowen Colthurst. Far from the men
being 'ringleaders', Sheehy Skeffington was a well-known
pacifist who had been trying to organise unofficial parties to
prevent looting in Dublin and the two other men, Thomas
Dickson and Patrick MacIntyre, were editors of 'violently
Loyalist papers which had strongly supported John
Redmond's recruiting campaign'.[31]

The privations of civilians feature in the contemporary
accounts. For some days the city was effectively paralysed
and food supplies quickly ran short.[32] Mrs Norway tells a
story of how 'Mrs. W.'s maid' walked forty miles carrying
meat and butter. 'Mrs. W.' was Elsie, wife of William Ireland
de Courcy Wheeler ('Dr. W.'), a prominent Dublin surgeon
who was knighted in 1919. Wheeler's brother, Major Henry
de Courcy Wheeler, was present when Patrick Pearse
formally surrendered at the end of the Rising.[33] In the
published version of her letters Mrs Norway referred to some
persons solely by initial, and it has been possible to identify
most of them. 'Dearest G.', to whom the letters were
addressed was Mrs Norway's sister, Grace. 'Lord S.' (first
mentioned on p. 45 below), Elsie Wheeler's father, was Lord
Shaw of Dunfermline, a law lord and formerly a Liberal M.P.,
who when he retired from the bench in 1929 became Lord
Craigmyle. Shaw was in Dublin recuperating from major
surgery (performed by his son-in-law) when he got caught up
in the Rising. Like many others in the city he could not resist
sight-seeing. 'No military regulation', he wrote in his
memoirs, was able to restrain 'the incredulous curiosity of the
populace'. Shaw also recalled 'a sense of relief and gratitude'
among the people 'when the military was poured into
Dublin' and he sentimentally remarked on 'their bravery and
good humour and courage, their kindness and friendship
towards the soldiery, and their mutual helpfulness'.[34] 'Mr. B.'
(p. 49) was Paul George Besson, manager of the Royal
Hibernian Hotel for many years; 'our friends the V.'s' (p. 51)

were William Henry Foster Verschoyle and his wife, who
lived at 36 Mount Street Upper. He was a chartered surveyor
and land agent. 'Sir M. N.' (p. 37) was Sir Matthew Nathan;
and Hamilton's loyal Post Office subordinate, 'Mr. C.' (p. 60)
was one of his principal clerks, John J. Coonan, whom her
husband singled out for particular mention in his memoir.
'Mr. O'B', who offered the Norways sanctuary after the
Rising at his country house, Celbridge Abbey, was Edmond
O'Brien, a wealthy and well-connected Catholic landowner.

In his memoir Norway describes how he had been
working at the G.P.O. on the morning of Easter Monday and
had been called away to a meeting with the Chief Secretary
at Dublin Castle just minutes before the insurgents occupied
the building. Norway speculated what might have been his
fate had he remained in the building just a few minutes
longer. Although at the outbreak of the war he had arranged
for a military guard to be provided at the Post Office, the
soldiers, curiously, had not been provided with any
ammunition for their guns. Two days before the Rising broke
out, Nevil, anxious about the general situation, had cleaned
and loaded his late brother Fred's automatic pistol and urged
his father to keep it by him. Norway himself, therefore, could
have been the only fully-armed official in the building. He
might, he thought, 'have tried to hold the staircase, and keep
the mob down … . The certain result', he continued with fine
irony, 'would have been that I should have been shot at once,
and the probable result would have been that the
Government in London would have declared the whole
trouble to have arisen from my wicked folly in firing on a
body of peaceful, if armed, citizens.' Both his memoir and his
wife's letters reflect the panic and confusion which swept
through the administration during the week. At the start of
the Rising, Sir Matthew Nathan, for whom Norway had no
high opinion, was reduced to shocked inaction. On the
Wednesday Norway was peremptorily called to the Vice-
Regal Lodge in Phoenix Park, and when no car could be

found, the Viceroy resorted to giving him instructions over the telephone in incomprehensible French. The next day Nathan summoned him four times to Dublin Castle 'without', as Norway complained, 'any reason of real advantage', though 'at some personal risk'. In the meantime, Norway, his wife and some brave and enterprising Post Office employees managed to keep the telegraph and some telephone services operating throughout the week.

Norway's memoir recounts the difficulties he had with the Dublin Castle authorities regarding their insouciant attitude towards revolutionary activity before the Rising, and, by contrast, the problems he also encountered concerning widespread, though unsubstantiated, allegations that the Post Office was riddled with Sinn Féiners. This opinion survives in popular historical memory. It is, for example, often asserted that, arising from his service in the Post Office, Michael Collins gained a special insight into British communications and how to intercept them.[35] Collins, in fact, from 1906–10 worked in the Post Office Savings Bank,[36] and so his expertise was more in the mysteries of double-entry bookkeeping than the secrets of the sorting office. In fact, very few of the seventeen thousand men and women in Norway's department proved to be disloyal. Norway told the Royal Commission on the Rebellion in Ireland that following the Rising only forty-eight people in the Postal Service had been found to be 'disloyal in various degrees. In some cases', he added, 'evidence was exceedingly slight.'[37] Before the Rising Norway had had some trouble with the O'Hegarty brothers, whom he describes in some detail. In August 1914, Patrick Sarsfield O'Hegarty (called 'Hegarty' in the memoir), the Postmaster of Queenstown (Cobh), County Cork, with a spotless Post Office record, came under military suspicion. Despite hesitations in London, Norway had him transferred to Whitchurch, Shropshire, where he prompted no further official concern.[38] Sometime later O'Hegarty's brother, Sean, also came under suspicion. Norway tried to transfer him from

Cork to England, but he chose dismissal instead. The suspicions about both brothers were fully confirmed after the war. P. S. O'Hegarty's book, *The Victory of Sinn Féin,* was published in 1924 and revealed, *inter alia,* that he had been a member of the Supreme Council of the Irish Republican Brotherhood, and Sean became a leading member of the Cork I.R.A. during the 1919–21 war. P. S. O'Hegarty resigned from the Post Office in 1918 and became a bookseller in Dublin. Norway does not relate (though he surely must have known) that after independence O'Hegarty was appointed Secretary of the Department of Posts and Telegraphs, thus becoming Norway's direct lineal bureaucratic successor.[39]

There is not much reflection as to the causes of the Rising in Mrs Norway's letters, though, as the *Times Literary Supplement* noticed, she had some caustic words for the Unionists who were preparing armed resistance to Home Rule before the Great War broke out. 'In Ulster', she wrote, 'the wind was sown, and my God, we have reaped the whirlwind!' Her account also reflects the contemporary (and erroneous) British assumption that the Rising owed more to German initiative than Irish. She assumed that Sinn Féin was 'encouraged no doubt by German intrigue and German money', and recorded armed Volunteers marching down Grafton Street singing 'Die Wacht am Rhein'. Nevil followed this line in his memoirs. 'The Germans', he wrote, 'established contact with the Sinn Fein volunteers by submarine and did everything within their power to stimulate a rising.' Their object was 'to cause the diversion of British troops from the Western Front. In this they were successful.'[40]

The most poignant feature of Mrs Norway's account concerns the fate of Fred's belongings, including his sword, which had been stored for safekeeping with other family valuables in Hamilton Norway's office safe and cupboard. Ironically Mrs Norway had thought it 'the safest place in Dublin'. Having inspected the burnt-out shell of the G.P.O. two days after the Rising had ended, she reflected sadly that everything belonging to 'F.' had gone. Later, however, some precious little treasures were recovered. Mrs Norway concluded that other things had been taken by the insurgents, though it is as likely that their property was simply swallowed up in the conflagration.

For Nevil, in Dublin for the school holidays, the Rising was a great adventure. 'This week', wrote his mother, 'has been a wonderful week for N. Never before has a boy of just seventeen had such an experience.' About half an hour after the G.P.O. had been seized, Nevil and his mother arrived in O'Connell (formerly Sackville) Street, on their way to meet his father for lunch. The street was crowded and 'there was a cordon of volunteers around the Post Office, and trigger-happy young men in green uniforms in great excitement were firing off their revolvers from time to time at nothing in particular'. Having sent his mother back to the hotel, Nevil witnessed the rebels attack a troop of lancers riding down O'Connell Street: 'These were the first men that I had seen killed'. He recalled that during the Rising 'I was far more comfortable and at home than my parents. This was my cup of tea. I was mentally conditioned for war; it was what I had been bred and trained for for two years.' He joined a Red Cross ambulance service organised by the Royal Irish Automobile Club and served as a stretcher bearer for most of the week.[41] With other medical workers the Order of St John of Jerusalem awarded him a 'Certificate of Honour' for his 'meritorious duty'.[42]

Although much of his writing has an autobiographical flavour and a number of his early novels clearly draw on his work as an aeronautical engineer, Shute made very little literary use of his Irish experiences. *Beyond the Black Stump,* published in 1956,[43] and sniffily dismissed by the *Times Literary Supplement* as 'a contrived and shallow piece of work',[44] is the only fiction in which he appears to have used any material from his time in Ireland. The novel concerns the relationship between Mollie Regan, one of a successful Irish-

Australian family running a large sheep station ('Laragh Station') in the remote north of Western Australia, near the Lunatic Mountains in the Hammersley Range, and Stanton Laird, an American geologist prospecting for oil. The main theme of the work lies in the contrast between the admirable qualities which Laird – a well-meaning if dull fellow – ascribes to the American frontier tradition and the actual frontier conditions which obtain at Laragh. The latter are characterised as lively, challenging and genuinely tolerant, in comparison to the steadier, more settled and less accommodating situation in the United States. Shute himself, an adventurous individualist, emigrated to Australia in the early 1950s, partly to escape the decadence, socialism and high taxation of post-war Britain, and certainly attracted by the freedom and opportunity available in his new home.

Laragh Station is owned by Pat and Tom Regan, both fervent Irish republicans who had fought with the IRA during the 1916 Rising and in the subsequent 'Troubles' of 1919–21. When they first emigrated to Australia and settled in the outback ('beyond the black stump', is an Australian expression meaning a remote place, or 'the back of beyond') they had, as Shute delicately put it, 'lived somewhat indiscriminately' with the local Aborigines, who at the time of the novel (the mid-1950s) still form part of the Laragh community. Pat's favourite, who ranked as the 'chief wife', is known as 'the Countess Markievicz' and there are (among others) two mixed-race sons called James Connolly and Joseph Plunkett. Having come under fire in St Stephen's Green, Dublin, where Constance Markievicz commanded a contingent of Volunteers, in his recollections of the Rising Arthur Hamilton Norway wrote of 'the virago, the Countess Markievicz'. Mrs Norway thought Markievicz had been 'one of the most dangerous of the leaders', and hoped that she would 'be treated with the same severity as the men'. Apart from the perhaps unintended surrealism, Shute may have been taking a quiet revenge for the ill-treatment he believed his family had received at the hands of the 1916 insurgents:

25

> The Countess was unaccustomed to a lavatory and her
> table manners had left much to be desired, so the men
> had fallen into the habit of dining alone while the black
> women took their meals out in the kitchen, or in any
> place they wished... The men ate in virtual silence;
> conversation at meal times was unknown on Laragh
> Station. The Countess slopped around in bare feet, huge,
> black, smiling, and shapeless in a cotton frock worn very
> evidently with nothing underneath it, removing used
> dishes from the table and carrying them out to wash.[45]

Shute's hint of animosity, or at least disapproval, towards the
1916 leaders is also echoed by a minor alteration he made in
his autobiographical reminiscences where he changed
'confusion' in the original typescript ('the sad confusion that
ended the rebellion') to 'sad atrocities and reprisals'.[46]

There are some other 'Irish' features in Shute's novel. Part
of the romantic interest turns on Mollie Regan's relationship
with David Cope, recently out from England and struggling
to make a success of a marginal, neighbouring property.
Cope's father had served not only in Gallipoli (providing 'a
close and obvious tie with the Australian forces'), but also in
the thuggish Black and Tans in Ireland after the First World
War. The Regans, naturally, are appalled to discover that
'that one's Dad was raising up the hand of murder against
poor boys fighting to drive out the English from their
country, and they with nothing but a rifle or maybe a hand
grenade itself to throw against machine guns in an armoured
car?' For a while it seems as if Cope will be ostracised, but the
Regans' tempers quickly cool. It is left to 'the Judge' – a
'drunken and disgraced old reprobate' who lives at Laragh
and provides for the author a source of intermittently wise
and learned commentary – to sum up the Regans as a
familiar Irish type: passionately exercised by historic wrongs,
yet also warm and sympathetic. 'They live much in the past,'
he observes, 'very much in the past. But they will grow

accustomed to the new idea, and they are both good-hearted men ... It will all pass.'[47]

Shute employs familiar national stereotypes in *Beyond the Black Stump*. Indeed, the strength of his fiction as a whole lies less in character development than with narrative power. Clearly mapped story-lines and vivid technical detail were what his loyal followers both expected and got. The Irish, thus, are slightly disreputable, living a warm, if somewhat unorthodox family life. But there was also a darker side to them. Perhaps recalling 1916, Shute has an Australian geologist, Donald Bruce, remark about the Regans: 'You may think them a queer lot, to start with. Take them the right way, and you'll find they can't do enough for you. Get their backs up, and they could be very troublesome.' Here Shute echoes his mother's description of the 'fine people' of Ireland: 'so kindly, so emotional, so clever, so easily guided, and so magnificent when wisely led'. Shute's Irish are notably hard drinkers. The Regans are shocked to discover that Stanton Laird does not take alcohol. 'They're very hospitable, you know, and that's about the only hospitality they understand', explains Bruce to Laird. 'They're really very nice people when you get to know them.' There is also a clear echo of the feckless stage Irishman in Tom Regan's complaint about the 'dastardly murdering' Black and Tans: 'Didn't they murder Jack Mullavy so, and he sleeping upon sentry in the glen with the rifle and the bottle at his side?'[48]

Part of the story of the Regans' haphazard personal relations has an Irish War of Independence twist. Mrs Regan, we learn, had originally been married to Tom Regan, by whom she had borne three children but had left him for his brother Pat, by whom she had Mollie. There had been no divorce, since, as Mollie put it, 'We're all Micks here'. As Catholics, divorce was impossible, and her parents' arrangement was merely de facto. Pat had softened Tom's feelings by presenting him with a cherished possession: 'General Shamus O'Brian's own Mauser that he carried at the start of the Troubles, in Easter Week 1916'. Both Regan brothers had been with O'Brian when he was killed on the roof of Jacob's biscuit factory.[49] Shute's original intention, however, had been for Pat to give Tom a racehorse, 'Laragh Lad', but this and some other details in the novel were changed after Shute's lawyers warned that his fictional characters might be identified with a real family, some of whose experiences the author had drawn on for his novel. To satisfy the lawyers, and avoid the possibility of a libel action, Shute proposed 'to substitute for the racehorse a relic of the Irish rebellion greatly prized by both brothers, such as a Mauser pistol used by Rory O'Connor in his last stand, or a crucifix carried by Pearse. To avoid offence in Ireland a fictitious hero might be used.'[50] So it was to be. Mollie explained the transaction to a baffled Stanton: 'I think perhaps it eased hard feelings when Daddy gave him the Mauser. There were just the three great Irish generals in the Troubles – Edmund [*sic*] Pearse, Rory O'Connor, and Shamus O'Brian, and Uncle Tom always says that O'Brian was the greatest of them all. The Mauser means an awful lot to them.'[51] No great offence on this score appears to have been taken in Ireland. The reviewer for the *Irish Independent* thought the background to the story was 'highly effective' and ambiguously praised the writer's 'excellent knowledge of stage-Irish dialogue'. He was less admiring of Shute's 'muddled knowledge of comparatively recent Irish history', which had resulted in some 'weird and wonderful' results.[52]

Shute's biographer claims that the 'Easter Rebellion', together with the Great War and 'his involvement in an exciting new industry', appear 'to have driven him to write'.[53] Whatever the case for the Great War, his experiences as a designer and builder of aircraft were certainly significant. But it is hard to find any direct evidence of a powerful Irish factor in his development or writing. Although Shute himself remarked that his time as a stretcher bearer had provided 'another push along the road to self-confidence',[54] he did not use that experience directly in any way at all. The frivolous marshalling forty years on of 'Irishry' in *Beyond the Black Stump* hardly constitutes much of a response. Yet in a more generalised way the 'Irish dimension' to his upbringing may have influenced his world-view. One critic has characterised Shute in his Australian years as an 'exile by choice' who found that in his adopted country there was 'still infinite possibility and challenge'. Within such an environment, moreover, Shute told story after story in which 'average men and women' possessing 'English virtues', such as honesty, self-sufficiency and responsibility, combined with technical competence, could 'achieve a great deal'.[55] Young Nevil Norway, one of an English family exiled in Ireland, an average boy thrown into an extraordinary situation, might fit this pattern. Another critic has observed that in his later novels Shute expounded his ideas 'within the framework of a "story of adventure" ... which typically achieved its dramatic effects by confronting an ordinarily decent and sturdy personality with some strange circumstances which required urgent, unaccustomed, and essentially developmental responses'.[56] Again, the pattern neatly fits the experience of Shute during the Easter Rising, so perhaps the inclusion of Ireland as an important factor in his development is not so fanciful after all. And, of course, some of the same analysis could be applied, exactly, to his mother's work, for what else is *The Sinn Fein Rebellion as I Saw It* if not the narrative of 'an ordinarily decent and sturdy personality' confronted with 'some strange and daunting circumstances'?

KEITH JEFFERY
Belfast, June. 1999

Introduction

NOTES

1. The *Official Index to The Times* covers all four editions; *Palmer's Index to The Times Newspaper* only refers to the final edition.
2. I am most grateful to Lindsay Duguid of the *Times Literary Supplement* who investigated this matter for me.
3. Obituary of Maj.-Gen. Gadsden, *The Times,* 28 Feb. 1899; entry for Edward Holroyd Gadsden (1859–1920) in *Who Was Who 1916–28.*
4. Nevil Shute, *Slide Rule: Autobiography of an Engineer* (Heinemann, London, 1954), p. 14.
5. As entered in the *British Library Catalogue.*
6. *The Times,* 3 Jan. 1939.
7. First published, respectively, in 1900, 1901 and 1931.
8. Julian Smith, *Nevil Shute (Nevil Shute Norway)* (Twane Publishers, Boston, 1976), p. 136. The *British Library Catalogue* lists 20 works by 'G. Norway'; the Library of Congress *National Union Catalog* erroneously ascribes them to 'George Norway'.
9. *The Times,* 3 Jan. 1939; Bernard Wasserstein, *Herbert Samuel* (Oxford University Press, Oxford, 1992), pp 120–1.
10. *The Times,* 9 Jan.1939.
11. Shute, *Slide Rule,* pp 7, 13.
12. R. B. McDowell, *The Irish Administration* (Routledge & Kegan Paul, London, 1964), pp 86–7.
13. Maurice Headlam, *Irish Reminiscences* (Robert Hale, London, 1947), p. 63.
14. See Wasserstein, *Herbert Samuel,* pp 129–46.
15. Statement read by Mr. A. H. Norway, 25 May 1916, *Royal Commission on the Rebellion in Ireland: Minutes of Evidence,* p. 61 [Cd. 8311] H. C. 1916, xi, 246.
16. See Lawrence W. McBride, *The Greening of Dublin Castle: the Transformation of Bureaucratic and Judicial Personnel in Ireland, 1892–1922* (Catholic University of America Press, Washington D.C., 1991).
17. Leon Ó Broin, *Dublin Castle and the 1916 Rising* (Sidwick & Jackson, London, 1970), pp 14-15. This, revised, edition of Ó Broin's book is much superior to the Helicon Press (Dublin) edition, published in 1966.
18. 10 Aug. 1912, quoted in McBride, *Greening of Dublin Castle,* p. 164.
19. 16 Aug. 1912, Healy to Maurice Healy (T. M. Healy, *Letters and Leaders of My Day* (Thornton Butterworth, London, 2 vols, 1928), vol. ii, p. 508).
20. Hobhouse to Sir Matthew Nathan, c. Feb. 1915, quoted in Ó Broin, *Dublin Castle,* p.48.
21. Norway to Nathan, 30 Sept. 1914, ibid., p. 15.
22. Healy, *Letters and Leaders of My Day,* ii, p. 508.
23. Shute, *Slide Rule,* p. 14. Addresses, and various other details, have been

extracted from contemporary issues of *Thom's Directory*.

24. He died on 4 July 1915. See Everard Wyrall, *The History of the Duke of Cornwall's Light Infantry, 1914–1919* (Methuen, London, 1932), pp 130, 479.
25. Shute, *Slide Rule*, p. 22.
26. Mrs Hamilton Norway, *The Sinn Fein Rebellion as I Saw It* (Smith, Elder, London, 1916), p. v.
27. James Stephens, *The Insurrection in Dublin* (Maunsel, Dublin, 1916).
28. *Letters from Dublin, Easter 1916: Alfred Fannin's Diary of the Rising*, ed. Adrian & Sally Warwick-Haller (Irish Academic Press, Dublin, 1995). Mrs Norway's account also illuminates the particular difficulties faced by Dublin hotels and their residents during the Rising. Cf. Elizabeth Bowen, *The Shelbourne* (Harrap, London, 1951), pp 151–62.
29. *Times Literary Supplement*, 10 Aug. 1916, p. 375.
30. Stephens, *Insurrection in Dublin*, p. 21. For rumours see also *Letters from Dublin*, pp 24–5, 42–3.
31. Max Caulfield, *The Easter Rebellion* (revised edition, Gill & Macmillan, Dublin, 1995), pp 153–4, 166–7.
32. See Stephens, *Insurrection in Dublin*, pp 60–1; *Letters from Dublin*, p. 32.
33. Caulfield, *The Easter Rebellion*, pp 348, 351.
34. Lord Craigmyle, *Letters to Isabel* (new edn, Nicholson & Watson, London, 1936), pp 286–90. Lord Macmillan's entry on Craigmyle in the *Dictionary of National Biography 1931–1940* warns that 'so far as it purports to narrate facts and to convey impressions', Craigmyle's memoir 'must be read with considerable reservations'. I am grateful to Dr Alan Bairner, of Dunfirmline and the University of Ulster at Jordanstown, for drawing my attention to this work.
35. See, for example, the entry on Collins in John Keegan & Andrew Wheatcroft (eds), *Who's Who in Military History* (Hutchinson, London, 1987), p. 76.
36. Tim Pat Coogan, *Michael Collins: A Biography* (Hutchinson, London, 1990), pp 15–17.
37. *Royal Commission on the Rebellion in Ireland: Minutes of Evidence*, p. 62 [Cd. 8311] H. C. 1916, xi, 247.
38. O'Hegarty himself indicates in his account of these times, *The Victory of Sinn Féin* (Talbot Press, Dublin, 1924), p. 16, that he was located in Welshpool, Montgomeryshire, so Norway may have been mistaken about Whitchurch.
39. Ronan Fanning says that O'Hegarty 'was the first head of a department appointed by the provisional government who, unlike the great majority of his colleagues, had not transferred from the British administration' (*The Irish Department of Finance 1922–58* (Institute of Public Administration, Dublin, 1978), pp 78–9). This, while strictly true, rather glosses over O'Hegarty's twenty-year career in the Post Office up to 1918.
40. Shute, *Slide Rule*, pp 23–4.

41. Ibid., pp 25–7.
42. *1916 Rebellion Handbook*, first published by the *Weekly Irish Times*, 1916 (Mourne River Press edn, Dublin, 1998), p. 237.
43. London: William Heinemann. Quotations below are taken from the first Australian edition (Heinemann, Melbourne, 1956).
44. 25 May 1956, p. 309.
45. *Beyond the Black Stump*, p. 81.
46. Typescript of 'Slide Rule' (Papers of Nevil Shute Norway (National Library of Australia), MS 2199 (henceforward Shute Papers), series 2, folder 16, f.12); Shute, *Slide Rule*, p. 24.
47. *Beyond the Black Stump*, pp 137–8.
48. Ibid., pp 73–4, 211.
49. Ibid., pp 119, 199.
50. See typescript of 'Beyond the Black Stump' and accompanying correspondence (Shute Papers, series 2, folder 17).
51. *Beyond the Black Stump*, p. 200.
52. *Irish Independent*, 2 June 1956.
53. Smith, *Nevil Shute*, p. 18.
54. Shute, *Slide Rule*, p. 26.
55. Jack W. Bennett, 'Nevil Shute – Exile by Choice', in Bruce Bennett (ed.), *A Sense of Exile: Essays in the Literature of the Asia-Pacific Region* (Centre for Studies in Australian Literature, University of Western Australia, Nedlands, W.A., 1988), pp 86–7.
56. Donald Lammers, 'Nevil Shute and the decline of the "Imperial Idea" in literature', *Journal of British Studies*, vol. xvi, no. 2 (Spring 1977), pp 124–5.

The Sinn Fein Rebellion
as I Saw It

MARY LOUISA HAMILTON NORWAY

The Sinn Fein Rebellion
as I Saw It

Royal Hibernian Hotel,
Dawson Street, Dublin

Tuesday, April 25th

DEAREST G., – I am afraid by this time you will have seen a good deal in the papers to cause you alarm, and as it is impossible to get a letter or telegram through, I will write you a detailed account of what we are going through and post it to you at the first opportunity.

To begin at the beginning, the Sinn Fein movement, which is now frankly revolutionary and which must not be confounded with Redmond's Nationalist Party, has been in existence for years, but has always been looked on as a small body of cranks who were thirsting for notoriety. Redmond's policy has always been to treat them with utter contempt, and the Government adopted his view. Since the outbreak of war this movement, encouraged no doubt by German intrigue and German money, has grown by leaps and bounds, and about eighteen months ago a large number broke away from Redmond's National Volunteers and formed a volunteer force which they called the Irish Volunteers. They are frankly and openly revolutionary, and when it became known some months ago that they were obtaining large quantities of arms and ammunition various persons did all they could to open the eyes of the authorities to the dangerous situation that was growing up. But as the explanation was always given that the force was for national defence only, the Government failed to take any steps to put down the movement.

During the past six months the body has grown enormously, as many as seven hundred recruits being enlisted on one night, and of course doing enormous harm to recruiting for the Army. On St. Patrick's Day they held a large review of several battalions, armed, and the trams were all held up for about an hour in College Green. Up to the last moment there was hope that this would be stopped, but protests were like a voice crying in the wilderness. Another time they held a full dress rehearsal of what has actually taken place when they "took" the Castle, St. Stephen's Green, and various buildings. About a month ago one of their meetings in the country was broken up and the two leaders arrested and deported to England. A huge meeting of protest was held at the Mansion House, almost opposite this hotel, and attended by the Volunteers, all armed, who marched in procession. After the meeting they marched down Grafton Street, singing "Die Wacht am Rhein" and revolutionary songs; a slight disturbance with the police took place and some shots were fired. People began to ask anxiously what next? but the Government looked on and smiled and H[amilton]. tore his hair.

On Saturday we were going to tea with friends at Bray, when just as we were starting H. got an "official" from the Castle, so I went alone and he went to the Castle. News had come that a boat had been taken off the Kerry coast, landing ammunition, and a very important arrest had been made. Easter Sunday passed off in absolute calm, and yesterday (Easter Monday) morning H. said he had a lot of letters to write and he would go and write them at his club, almost next door to the Sackville Street G.P.O. He found he wanted to

answer some letters that were in his desk at the G.P.O., so he
walked over to his room and was just sitting down when his
'phone went, an urgent message to go at once to the Castle.
He had only just arrived there, and was in consultation
with Sir M[atthew]. N[athan]., when suddenly a volley of
shots rang out at the Castle gate, and it was found armed
bodies of men were in possession of the City Hall and other
houses that commanded the other gates to the Castle, and
anyone attempting to leave the Castle was shot. All the
officials in the Castle were prisoners.

News quickly came that the magazine in the Park had
been taken, the G.P.O., two stations, and all the houses that
commanded O'Connell Bridge had been stormed and taken,
and the rebels had taken St. Stephen's Green, where they
were entrenching themselves.

Meantime, knowing nothing of this, N[evil]. went for a
country motor bike ride, and I did some sewing and wrote
letters, etc., and when N. came in about 12.30 I said I wanted
a walk before lunch and we would walk down to the club and
meet H. The streets were quiet and deserted till we crossed
O'Connell Bridge, when N. remarked there was a dense
crowd round Nelson's Pillar, but we supposed it was a bank
holiday crowd waiting for trams. We were close to the
General Post Office when two or three shots were fired,
followed by a volley, and the crowd began rushing down
towards the bridge, the people calling, out "Go back, go back;
the Sinn Feiners are firing." N. said, "You'd better go back,
Mother; there's going to be a row; I'll go on to the club and
find Dad"; so I turned and fled with the crowd and got back
safely to the hotel.

Here was excitement and consternation. Every moment
people were coming in with tales of civilians being shot in the
streets, and houses commanding wide thoroughfares and
prominent positions being taken possession of by the Sinn
Feiners, whose method was to go in detachments of four or
six armed men, ring the bell, and demand to see the owners

of the houses. In many instances they were away for the Easter holidays, when the frightened servants were just turned into the street to go where they would; but if the master or mistress were at home they were told with a revolver at their heads that the house was required by the Irish Republic for strategic purposes, and the owners were given the option of leaving the house or remaining as prisoners in the basement. A few elected to do this in preference to leaving all their household goods to the mercy of the rebels; but most thought "discretion the better part of valour" and cleared out to friends, in some instances only to be hunted out from their house of refuge a second time. The windows of the houses were then barricaded with a reckless disregard to valuable furniture, which in many cases was turned into the street to form barricades.

You remember my nice housemaid Mary, gentle as a dove and timid as a hare. I had got her a very nice place with a lady who had taken a large house in Leeson Street close to the bridge and commanding Fitzwilliam Place. She went this morning by appointment to meet the lady at the house and found the Sinn Feiners on the steps, who pointed their revolvers at her and told her to clear out. She was so scared she nearly fell into the area, and came to the hotel looking like a ghost.

But to return to our own adventures. Directly I got back to the hotel I rang up the club and was told by old MacDermott, the hall-porter, that H. had left the club at 11.30 to go to the G.P.O., saying he would be back shortly; but he had not returned, and since then the Post Office had been stormed and the guard shot or overpowered, and the Sinn Feiners were in possession of the whole building, and firing volleys on the police from the windows! Imagine my feelings!

About 1.30 N. returned, having failed to find any trace of H., but he had seen some cavalry shot coming out of Talbot Street into Sackville Street. The first three or four were just picked off their horses and fell wounded or dead, and the horses were shot. He said the scene of excitement in Sackville Street was indescribable. We were just going in to lunch when a telephone message came through saying H. was at the Castle but could not leave.

This relieved our minds as to his fate, and after lunch I was kept busy at the telephone answering distracted messages from Post Office officials who were wandering about looking for H. At about 4 p.m. N. returned from a tour of inspection, and told me all was quiet in Sackville Street, and begged me to go out with him and see the G.P.O.

I quaked rather, but we set off and reached Sackville Street safely.

Over the fine building of the G.P.O. floated a great green flag with the words "Irish Republic" on it in large white letters. Every window on the ground floor was smashed and barricaded with furniture, and a big placard announced "The Headquarters of the Provisional Government of the Irish Republic." At every window were two men with rifles, and on the roof the parapet was lined with men. H.'s room appeared not to have been touched, and there were no men at his windows.

We stood opposite and were gazing, when suddenly two shots were fired, and, seeing there was likely to be an ugly rush, I fled again, exhorting N. to take refuge at the club.

He never reached the club, but came back to the hotel, and we had tea, and he then went to inspect St. Stephen's Green.

He found all round the Green, just inside the railings among the shrubberies, the rebels had dug deep pits or holes, and in every hole were three men. They had barricaded the street opposite the Shelbourne Hotel, and there had been a lot of firing and several people killed, and shots had gone into the hotel, which is, as you know, a fine building facing the Green.

All the evening we heard firing in all directions of the city and rumours of troops having arrived from the Curragh.

While at dinner another message came through from H. to say we were not to be alarmed; he was quite safe, but might not get home that night.

After dinner N. went out to see if he could get near the Castle, but he found awful fighting. The troops were storming the City Hall and using machine-guns, and it was too "unhealthy" for him to get near, so he came back at 9 and went to bed.

I stayed up in case of being wanted on the 'phone, and at 11.30 p.m. went up to my room, and a few minutes later H. walked in, to my immense relief.

The troops had arrived from the Curragh at about 5 p.m. and had promptly stormed the City Hall, which commanded the main gate of the Castle, and had taken it after fierce fighting.

H. saw prisoners being brought into the Castle yard, and when all was quiet he and several other officials crept out and reached their various homes.

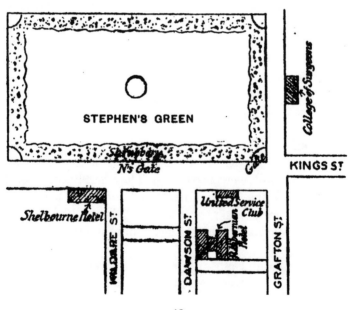

People are appalled at the utter unpreparedness of the Government. In the face of a huge body of trained and armed men, openly revolutionary, they had taken no precautions whatever for the defence of the city in the event of an outbreak. At the beginning of the war H. obtained a military guard, armed, for the G.P.O., and they have always been there. When the outbreak occurred yesterday the armed guard were there, but with no ammunition! The sergeant was wounded in two places and the rest overpowered.

All night the firing continued. Between 1 and 2 a.m. it was awful, and I lay and quaked. It was all in the direction of the Castle.

This morning we hear the military are pouring into the city, and are in the Shelbourne Hotel and Trinity College.

The rebels have barricaded Sackville Street, and it is expected to be very fierce fighting over the G.P.O. It is terrible!

All our valuables were stored in H.'s safe and cupboard when we gave up our house, and all our dear F[red].'s books, sword, and all his possessions, which we value more than anything else in the world. We would not trust them with the stored furniture.

Yesterday afternoon the mob broke all the windows in various streets and looted all the shops. The streets were strewn with clothes, boots, furniture, tram cushions, and everything you can imagine.

While I am writing now there is incessant firing in St. Stephen's Green, and we fear there may be street fighting in this street.

In case you have forgotten, I will put a little plan here [see p. 40].

Tuesday, 5 p.m.

This morning martial law was proclaimed (I will try and get a copy of the proclamation) at 11.30 and the rebels given four hours to surrender.

A cruiser and two transports are said to have arrived at Kingstown, with troops from England. At 3.30 p.m., as there had been no surrender, the troops started to clear St. Stephen's Green, and raked it with machine-guns from the top of the Shelbourne Hotel and the United Service Club. We hear there are many casualties. N. has just come in, and says a big fire is raging in Sackville Street in the shops opposite the G.P.O., supposed to have been caused by the mob finding fireworks in a toy shop. The fire brigade arrived almost at once and could easily have overcome the fire, but the brigade was fired on by the Sinn Feiners, making it impossible for them to bring the engines into action, and they had to beat a retreat and leave the shops to burn themselves out. N. says the troops are clearing the houses of rebels behind Dame Street and the region of the Castle, and there is a lot of firing. It has turned to rain, which has cleared the streets of people.

A telegram has just come from the Admiralty stopping the mail boat from crossing. No boat has gone to-day, and we are absolutely cut off.

All the roads leading out of Dublin are in the hands of the rebels.

H. and N. have just come in, having seen Dr. W[heeler]. (now Major W.), Surgeon to the Forces in Ireland. He told them that so far we had had about 500 casualties, two-thirds of them being civilians, shot in the streets.

The first thing Dr. W. heard of the outbreak was a 'phone message telling him to go at once to the Shelbourne as a man had been shot. He supposed it was a case of suicide, so jumped into his car and went off, fortunately in mufti. In Nassau Street his car was stopped and he was ordered to get out by rebels. He attempted to argue, and was told if he did not obey instantly he would be shot. Had he been in uniform he would have been shot at sight. As a civilian doctor they allowed him to go, and he took his bag and ran. He found three men shot in the Shelbourne, and a boy was shot as he reached the door.

Wednesday, April 26th, 9.30 a.m.

Last evening was quiet till we went to bed at 10.30, when almost immediately a furious machine-gun fire began. It seemed just at the back of the hotel, but was really at the top of Grafton Street and the street leading to Mercer's Hospital. It lasted about twenty minutes, and then almost immediately after we got into bed a 'phone came that H. was to go at once to the Vice-Regal Lodge in the Phoenix Park, so he dressed and tried every way to get a motor; but of course no motor would go out. After some delay he got the field ambulance of the fire brigade at Dr. W.'s suggestion; but when it came the men told H. they had been carrying wounded all day, and that they had been constantly stopped by pickets and the car searched, and if they went and the car was stopped and found to contain H. they would undoubtedly all be shot; so H. considered it too risky, and it had to be abandoned. Eventually his Excellency gave his instructions over the 'phone, first in French, but that particular 'phone either did not speak or did not understand French; so eventually he took the risk of the 'phone being tapped and gave them in English. At last H. got to bed about 1 a.m., to be at the 'phone again at 5 a.m.

While we were dressing a terrific bombardment with field guns began – the first we had heard – and gave me cold shivers. The sound seemed to come from the direction of the G.P.O., and we concluded they were bombarding it. It went on for a quarter of an hour – awful! big guns and machine-guns – and then ceased, but we hear they were bombarding

Liberty Hall, the headquarters of Larkin and the strikers two years ago, and always a nest of sedition. It is now crammed with Sinn Feiners. The guns were on H.M.S. *Helga,* that came up the river and smashed it from within about three hundred yards. It made me feel quite sick.

We think that they are leaving the Post Office for a time with the hope that when other strongholds are taken the Republican Government will surrender. H. has just been summoned to the Castle, and there is no knowing when he will be back. All who go out carry their lives in their hands. I went out twice yesterday, but we were turned back by shots being fired from upper windows, and the Lord Lieutenant has issued a proclamation begging people to keep in their houses, so I must restrain my curiosity.

All the shops remain closed, and no papers are issued except the proclamation, and we know nothing of what is going on in other parts of Ireland. But there are wild rumours of insurrection in Cork and other places.

This morning there is firing again in St. Stephen's Green, so the rebels are still there.

N. did a very fine thing yesterday. After the Green had been raked by our machine-gun fire he strolled up, in his casual way, to see the result! In front of one of the side gates in the railings, which are seven feet high and spiked three ways, he saw a small group of men peering into the Green. He went to see what they were looking at. The rebels had barricaded the gate, which opened inwards, by putting one of the heavy garden seats against it *upside down* and on the top of it another *right side up,* and lying full length on the seat, face downwards, was a man, a civilian, with all his lower jaw blown away and bleeding profusely. N. immediately climbed the railings and dropped down on the Sinn Fein side and found that the man was still living; he then turned and fairly cursed the men who were looking on, and asked if there was not one man enough to come over the railings and help him. Whereupon three men climbed over and together they lifted down the seat with the poor creature on it, dragged away the other seat, when they were able to open the gate, and then brought out the seat and the man on it and carried him to the nearest hospital, where he died in about five minutes.

N.'s theory is he was probably one of the civilians taken prisoner by the Sinn Fein the previous day, and was trying to escape from the awful machine-gun fire when he was shot down and fell back on to the seat. It was a terrible case.

The rebels from St. Stephen's Green are now also in possession of the College of Surgeons and are firing across the Green at the troops in the Shelbourne Hotel.

Lord S[haw]. tells me that 30,000 troops were landed at Kingstown this morning, and we hear they are amazed at their reception, as they had been told that they were going to quell a rebellion in Ireland, and lo! on their arrival at Kingstown the whole population turned out to cheer them, giving them food, cigarettes, chocolate, and everything the hospitable inhabitants could provide, so that the puzzled troops asked plaintively: "Who then are we going to fight, and where is the rebellion?" However, they were quickly disillusioned, for in marching into Dublin, when they reached Ballsbridge they came within range of several houses occupied by Sinn Feiners, and without a word of warning the battalion of Sherwood Foresters came under terrible cross-fire and were just shot down, unable to return a single shot. I have not heard how many casualties occurred, but two or three officers and many men were killed and a number wounded. So surely soon we must be relieved.

Thursday, April 27th

Last night the mail boat left carrying passengers, and if it goes this evening Lord S. may be crossing, and he will take this to you.

Yesterday afternoon and evening there was terrible fighting. The rebels hold all the bridges over the canal, one on the tram line between this and Blackrook, another at the end of Baggot Street, and the other at Leeson Street. The fighting was terrible, but in the end we took the Leeson Street bridge, and I hope still hold it, as this opens a road to Kingstown. We failed to take the other two.

At the end of Lower Mount Street the rebels held the schools, and there was fierce fighting: our troops failed to surround the schools, and in the end, when they at last took them by a frontal attack with the loss of eighteen men and one officer, only one rebel was taken, the rest having escaped by the back.

Yesterday, to our great indignation, the public-houses were allowed to be open from 2 till 5, though every shop, bank, and public building was closed – just to inflame the mob, it could not have been on any other grounds; and yet at 8 p.m., after being on duty from 5 a.m., H. could not get a whiskey and soda, or even a glass of cider with his dinner, as it was out of hours. I was *furious!*

I must close this, as Lord S. has come in and says he expects to go to-night and will take this and H.'s report, so I will start a fresh letter to-morrow.

Don't worry overmuch about us. We quite expect to come out of this, but if we don't N. is *yours.*

L. N.

SECOND LETTER

Friday, 10 *a.m.*

DEAREST G., – After all my letter did not get off last night, as the roads were too dangerous to admit of Dr. W. motoring

Lord S. to Kingstown. He got a permit to pass our troops, but there were too many Sinn Fein positions and snipers to make it possible for them to pass through.

If the position improves, he will go tonight, so I may be able to send this too, if I can write enough to make it worth while, but I am still rather shaky from a fright I had last night.

Yesterday morning the Red Cross ambulance sent in to the hotel to ask for volunteer workers to act as stretcher-bearers and do all sorts of jobs connected with the Red Cross, and N. and several men staying in the hotel volunteered. I was glad he should, as he is of course safer attached to the Red Cross than roaming the streets making rescues on his own, and if he was killed or wounded we should at least hear of it. But the risks are many and great, as in this kind of street fighting, where all the firing is from windows or from house-tops, the ambulance are frequently under fire.

However, N. having volunteered promptly went off, and we saw him no more. While we were having dinner Mr. O'B[rien]., who had been out all day with the ambulance, was dining with us. H. was called to the telephone to receive this message: "You must not expect to see or hear from me till this is over."

H. asked who the message was from, and the answer came back: "Your son," in a voice that H. was sure was not N.'s. H. then asked where the message came from, and was told "The Castle."

He returned to us greatly perturbed, and we held a consultation. We all agreed there was only one interpretation to be put on it, viz., that N. had been taken prisoner by the rebels, and that someone who was well disposed to H. had taken this opportunity of letting him know, and that saying the message came from the Castle was just a blind. H. rang up the head of the Red Cross, and he told us only two of the Red Cross volunteers were missing who had been out that day, and both of them were known, and N. was not one of them, so we were still more mystified.

It then occurred to H. that it might be possible to trace back the message and find out where it really had been sent from, so he called up the exchange, and after a little delay he heard the message had actually been sent from the Castle and by N., who was there.

Imagine our relief! though still completely in the dark as to why the boy had not come back like other workers, and why we were not to expect to see him again.

Next morning in walked the truant, not best pleased that we had been inquiring for him. His explanation was quite simple. He had been attached to a branch of the ambulance that had its depôt at the Castle, so worked from there and returned to the Castle at night. Hearing this, and not knowing in the least to what part of the city his work would take him, and the impossibility of sending any message or note to tell us where he was, and knowing how anxious I should be if he did not return, he asked the Castle authorities if he might send a message to *relieve our minds!* He was told he might do so, but it must only be one sentence, and he must have the censor in the box with him. This so flustered N. that he could think of nothing to say but the words I have quoted; they seemed to him to express the position exactly, and he never dreamt of the interpretation we should put on them. As it was I spent an hour I don't ever like to remember and which unnerved me more than I thought possible, and all I got was a trouncing from N. for being so "nervy." Surely much is expected from mothers these days!

The volunteer workers, among other things, enter houses where there are known to be wounded Sinn Feiners and bring them out and take them to hospitals.

This N. was doing yesterday. One of the most awful things in this terrible time is that there must be scores of dead and dying Sinn Feiners, many of them mere lads, that no one can get at in the houses, and where they will remain till after the rebellion; and in some cases the houses take fire and they are all burnt. However, whatever is possible is being done.

Yesterday was the worst day we have had, as there was desperate fighting in Grafton Street, just at our back, and the side streets; and several volleys in our street.

In the morning I was sitting on a settee near the window of the lounge, knitting and looking out and listening to the firing in Grafton Street, when shots were fired just outside our windows, and Mr. B[esson]., the manager, came in and said, "We must shut all the shutters, Mrs. N., it is getting a bit too hot, and I am taking no risks." So all the shutters were closed, and I moved to the drawing-room above, which also overlooks the street.

All the afternoon an awful battle raged in the neighbourhood of the river and quays, and the din of the great guns and machine-guns was tremendous. We now have 30,000 troops and plenty of artillery and machine-guns, so the result cannot be uncertain, though there is desperate work to be done before the end is in sight.

The troops are said to have formed a huge semi-circle with the G.P.O. as the centre, and, starting from the river, are driving the rebels back street by street, till eventually they will be in a small enclosure, when they will bombard it to pieces.

The G.P.O. has such valuable records, etc., and the contents of the safes are so precious, that they will not raze it to the ground if they can help it; but it has so much subterranean space, that would afford cover to thousands of Sinn Feiners, that we hear they are going to fire some "gas" shells into it and then rush it!

Up to yesterday afternoon they had got to Abbey Street on the right, and no doubt were closing in equally on other sides. The shells had started several fires; nearly all the shops on the quay on the side of the Custom House were burning yesterday afternoon, and later in the evening many others broke out.

I cannot give you any idea of what it was like when I went to bed. I sent for Mrs. B., the manager's wife, such a splendid

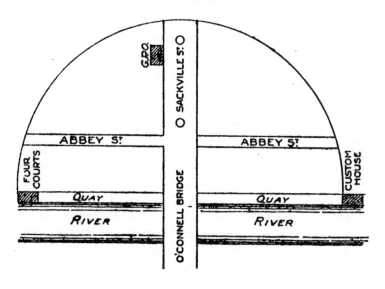

little woman, and together we watched it from my window, which is high up and looked in the right direction.

It was the most awe-inspiring sight I have ever seen. It seemed as if the whole city was on fire, the glow extending right across the heavens, and the red glare hundreds of feet high, while above the roar of the fires the whole air seemed vibrating with the noise of the great guns and machine-guns. It was an inferno! We remained spell-bound, and I can't tell you how I longed for you to see it. We had only just come down from the window – we had been standing on the window ledge leaning out – when H. came and told us no one was to look out of the windows as there was cross-firing from the United Service Club and another building, and Mr. O'B., who was watching the fires from his window, had a bullet a few inches from his head!!

About 2 a.m. I woke to find the room illuminated in spite of dark blinds and curtains, and I rushed to the window and saw an enormous fire; it seemed to be in the direction of the Four Courts, which is in the hands of the Sinn Feiners, and we hear this morning that a portion of the buildings was burnt last night.*

Yesterday Lord S. had a narrow escape from a sniper who has been worrying this street for two days and could not be located. He was picking off soldiers during the fighting in Grafton Street, but later turned his attention to the cross streets between this and Grafton Street, and there as nearly as possible got Lord S., who was coming back to us from the Castle.

The military thought the man was on *our* roof, which made us all bristle with indignation – the mere idea of the wretch being on our hotel; but a thorough search proved he was not here, though he evidently had access to *some* roof.

In this respect we are much better off than our friends the V[erschoyle].'s. They came into their town house only about a month ago, and being in Upper Mount Street it was in one of the most active haunts of the snipers. They had several on their roof, and when they went up to bed at night they could hear the snipers walking about and talking on the roof. Does it not make one creep to think of it? Mr. V. had his bed put on the upper landing exactly under the trap-door on to the roof, so that had the rebels attempted to enter the house at night they would have come down "plop" on to him in his bed. He surrounded himself with all the arms he could muster, and the wretched Mrs. V. lay in bed and quaked, expecting any minute to hear a battle royal raging outside her bedroom door. In this street an old lady of seventy-three was shot through the leg in her own room, and was taken to Dr. W.'s home, where she had to have her leg amputated; and in another house a servant flashed on her electric light when going to bed and was instantly shot through the head! Our friend Miss K. also had a narrow escape. She had only just left her drawing-room, when a bullet passed straight through the room and buried itself in a picture.

---

*This was incorrect; it was the Linen Hall barracks that were burnt.

Yesterday afternoon, when the firing in Grafton Street was over, the mob appeared and looted the shops, clearing the great provision shops and others. From the back of this hotel you look down on an alley that connects with Grafton Street, – and at the corner, the shop front in Grafton Street, but with a side entrance into this lane, is a very large and high-class fruiterer. From the windows we watched the proceedings, and I never saw anything so brazen! The mob were chiefly women and children with a sprinkling of men. They swarmed in and out of the side door bearing huge consignments of bananas, the great bunches on the stalk, to which the children attached a cord and ran away dragging it along. Other boys had big orange boxes which they filled with tinned and bottled fruits. Women with their skirts held up received showers of apples and oranges and all kinds of fruit which were thrown from the upper windows by their pals; and ankle-deep on the ground lay all the pink and white and silver paper and paper shavings used for packing choice fruits. It was an amazing sight, and nothing daunted these people. Higher up at another shop we were told a woman was hanging out of a window dropping down loot to a friend, when she was shot through the head by a sniper, probably our man; the body dropped into the street and the mob cleared. In a few minutes a hand-cart appeared and gathered up the body, and instantly all the mob swarmed back to continue the joyful proceedings!

H. and Lord S. were sitting at the window for a few minutes yesterday when the fruit shop was being looted, and saw one of the funniest sights they had ever seen. A very fat, very blousy old woman emerged from the side street and staggered on to the pavement laden with far more loot than she could carry. In her arms she had an orange box full of fruit, and under her shawl she had a great bundle tied up which kept slipping down. Having reached the pavement, she put down her box and sat on it, and from her bundle rolled forth many tins of fruit. These she surveyed ruefully, calling on the Almighty and all the saints to help her!! From these she solemnly made her selection, which she bound up in her bundle and hoisted, with many groans and lamentations, on her back and made off with, casting back many longing looks at the pile of things left on the pavement, which were speedily disposed of by small boys.

On Wednesday when the looting was going on in Sackville Street a fine, large boot shop was receiving attention from swarms of looters. Ragged women and children were seen calmly sitting in the window trying on boots and shoes, and one old woman with an eye to future needs made up a bundle of assorted sizes and tied them up in her apron. She had only reached the pavement, when she bethought her to leave her bundle in a corner and return for a further consignment which she tied up in her shawl. On returning to the street great was her rage and indignation on finding the original bundle had disappeared. Then were there sore lamentations and violent abuse of the police, who could not even "protect the property of a poor old woman."

In Sackville Street was a very large shop called Clery's; for some reason the looters were afraid to start on it; and old women passed up and down gazing longingly at fur coats and silken raiment and saying sorrowfully, "Isn't Clery's broke yet?" and "Isn't it a great shame that Clery's is not broke!" Rumour and tragedy are so intermixed in this catastrophe. A very delicate elderly lady who is staying here said to me this morning, in answer to my inquiry as to how she had slept: "I could not sleep at all. When the guns ceased the *awful silence* made me so nervous!" I know exactly what she meant. When the roar of the guns ceases you can *feel* the silence.

4 p.m.

When I had got so far this morning I got an urgent message from the Red Cross asking me to make more armlets for the workers. With two other ladies I had been making them yesterday, so I collected my helpers and we worked till lunch, when another request came that we would make four large Red Cross flags, as they were going to try to bury some of the dead and needed the flags for the protection of the parties. We have just finished them, and are wondering what will be the next call. It is such a good thing I have my sewing-machine here.

On Wednesday evening Lord S. was at Mercer's Hospital with a doctor when eleven dead were brought in, and a priest brought in a rifle he had taken from a dead Sinn Feiner. It had an inscription in German and the name of the factory in Berlin, which Lord S. copied. It is believed that nearly all the arms and ammunition are of German make, and it is said that the cruiser that was sunk on Saturday was bringing heavy guns and forty officers, but I don't know if there is any truth in that. The opinion is very strong that the Sinn Feiners were led to believe that they would have great German reinforcements, and that all they had to do was to hold the troops here for a couple of days while the Germans landed a big force on the west coast of Ireland. We also hear that Sir R. Casement has been shot in London, but you probably know a great deal more about that than I do, as we see no papers and are completely cut off from all news.

On Wednesday three of the ringleaders were caught, and it is said they were shot immediately! It is also believed that Larkin was shot on the top of a house in St Stephen's Green, but as the rebels still hold the house it has not been possible to identify him, but he is said to have been here on Monday.*

---

*This was incorrect; it appears Larkin was not in Dublin.

5 p.m.

Colonel C. has just come in, having been in the thick of it for forty-eight hours. He tells us the Post Office has been set on fire by the Sinn Feiners, who have left it. If this is true, and it probably is, I fear we have lost all our valuable possessions, including my diamond pendant, which was in my jewel-case in H.'s safe.

To-day about lunch-time a horrid machine-gun suddenly gave voice very near us. We thought it was in this street, but it may have been in Kildare Street; also the sniper reappeared on the roofs, and this afternoon was opposite my bedroom window judging from the sound. I pulled down my blinds. A man might hide for weeks on the roofs of these houses among the chimney stacks and never be found as long as he had access to some house for food. When we were working in my room this afternoon he fired some shots that could not have been more than twenty yards away.

The serious problem of food is looming rather near, as nothing has come into the city since Saturday. Boland's bakery, an enormous building, is in the hands of the rebels, who have barricaded all the windows with sacks of flour, and it is said it will have to be blown up. There is not a chance of getting them out in any other way. The rebels also have Jacob's biscuit factory, where there are still huge stores of flour. Every prominent building and every strategic position was taken before the authorities at the Castle woke to the fact that there was a rebellion!

I was almost forgetting to tell you how splendidly one of H.'s men behaved when the G.P.O. was taken. When the rebels took possession they demanded the keys from the man who had them in charge. He quietly handed over the keys, having first abstracted the keys of H.'s room!

Imagine such self-possession at such a terrible moment.

A young man has come to stay in the hotel who saw the taking of the G.P.O. He was staying at the hotel exactly opposite the building and went into the G.P.O. to get some stamps. As he was leaving the office a detachment of about fifteen Irish Volunteers marched up and formed up in front of the great entrance. He looked at them with some curiosity, supposing they were going to hold a parade; two more detachments arrived, and immediately the word of command was given, and they rushed in through the door. Shots were fired inside the building, and, as the young man said, he "hooked it" back to the hotel, which was one of those burnt a few days later. The whole thing occupied only a few moments, as, being Bank Holiday, there was only a small staff in the building.

6.30 *p.m.*

A party of soldiers and a young officer have just arrived to search the roof for the sniper. They say he is on the roof of the annexe, which is connected with the main building by covered-in bridges. They are now on the roof and shots are being fired, so I expect they have spotted him.

When N. was out last night another ambulance had a bad experience. They had fetched three wounded Sinn Feiners out of a house, and were taking them to hospital, when they came under heavy fire. The driver was killed, so the man beside him took the wheel and was promptly wounded in both legs. The car then ran away and wrecked itself on a lamp post. Another ambulance had to run the gauntlet and go to the rescue!

On the whole as far as possible the rebels have respected the Red Cross, but not the white flag. In house-to-house fighting there can be no connected action, and yesterday when a house was being stormed the rebels hung out a white flag, and when the troops advanced to take them prisoners they were shot down from a house a few doors higher up the street, so now no more white flag signals are to be recognised.

If they want to surrender they must come out and take their own risks.

We asked N. if he knew what had happened to the ambulance that had two men missing yesterday, and he told us they were in the act of entering a Sinn Fein house to bring out wounded with two other men when the ambulance came under such heavy fire that, as it contained one or two other wounded men, it had to beat a retreat and moved off. Two of the volunteer helpers ran after it and succeeded in reaching it and climbed in, but the other two took refuge in the area, and N. did not know how or when they were rescued. This is an instance of the extreme danger that attends the ambulance work. The marvel is that the casualties are so few.

Guinness's Brewery have made three splendid armoured cars by putting great long boilers six feet in diameter on to their large motor lorries. Holes are bored down the sides to let in air, and they are painted grey. The driver sits inside too. They each carry twenty-two men or a ton of food in absolute security. N. saw them at the Castle being packed with men; nineteen got in packed like herrings, and three remained outside. Up came the sergeant: "Now then, gentlemen, move up, move up: the car held twenty-two yesterday; it must hold twenty-two to-day"; and in the unfortunate three were stuffed. It must have been suffocating, but they were taken to their positions in absolute safety.

Saturday, 29th, 10 a.m.

Last night was an agitating one. The sniper was very active, and after dinner several shots struck the annexe, one or two coming through the windows, and one broke the glass roof of the bridge. Mr. B., who never loses his head, decided to get all the people out of the annexe, with staff (about forty people); and all we in the main building, whose rooms look out on the back, were forbidden to have lights in our rooms at all. There was such a strong feeling of uneasiness throughout the hotel, and always the danger of its being set on fire, that about 10 p.m. H. said we must be prepared at any moment to leave the hotel if necessary. So we went up to our room and in pitch darkness groped about and collected a few things (F.'s miniature and the presentation portrait of him, my despatch case with his letters, my fur coat, hat and boots), and we took them down to the sitting-room, which H. uses as an office, on the first floor. All the people in the hotel were collected in the lounge, which is very large and faces the street, and the whole of the back was in complete darkness. The firing quieted down, and about 11.30 we crept up to our room and lay down in our clothes. When dawn broke I got up and undressed and had two hours' sleep. All the rest of the guests spent the night in the lounge.

This morning we hear an officer has been to say that the shots fired into the hotel last night were fired by the military. People were constantly pulling up their blinds for a moment with the lights on to look at the city on fire, and the military have orders to fire on anything that resembles signalling without asking questions.

Reliable news has come in this morning that nothing remains of the G.P.O. but the four main walls and the great portico. It is absolutely burnt out. The fires last night were terrible, but we dared not look out. Eason's Library and all the shops and buildings between O'Connell Bridge and the G.P.O. on both sides of Sackville Street are gone.

It is difficult to think of the position without intense bitterness, though God knows it is the last thing one wishes for at such a time. In pandering to Sir E. Carson's fanaticism and allowing him to raise a body of 100,000 armed men for the sole purpose of rebellion and provisional government the Government tied their own hands and rendered it extremely difficult to stop the arming of another body of men, known to be disloyal, but whose *avowed* reason was the internal defence of Ireland! In Ulster the wind was sown, and, my God, we have reaped the whirl-wind!

We hear that many of our wounded are being sent to Belfast, as the hospitals here are crowded, and the food problem must soon become acute. Mr. O'B. told me his ambulance picked up four wounded, three men and a woman, and took them to the nearest hospital. The woman was dying, so they stopped at a church and picked up a priest; arrived at the hospital the authorities said they could not possibly take them in as they had not enough food for those they had already taken, but when they saw the condition of the woman they took her in to die, and the others had to be taken elsewhere.

If the main walls of the G.P.O. remain standing it may be we shall find the safe in H.'s room still intact. It was built into the wall, and my jewel-case was in it, but all our silver, old engravings, and other valuables were stored in the great mahogany cupboards when we gave up our house in the autumn, as being the safest place in Dublin.

4 *p.m.*

Sir M. N. has just rung up to say the rebels have surrendered unconditionally. We have no details, and the firing continues in various parts of the town. But if the leaders have surrendered it can only be a question of a few hours before peace is restored, and we can go forth and look on the wreck and desolation of this great city.

So ends, we hope, this appalling chapter in the history of Ireland – days of horror and slaughter comparable only to the Indian Mutiny. This seems a suitable place, dear G., to end this letter, and I hope to start a happier one to-morrow.

Yours,

L. N.

THIRD LETTER

Sunday, April 30th, 10 a.m.

DEAREST G., – When I closed my letter last night with the news that the rebel leaders had surrendered I hoped to start this new letter in a more cheerful strain; but while we were dining last night H. was rung up from the Castle to hear that the whole of Sackville Street north of the G.P.O. right up to the Rotunda was on fire and blazing so furiously that the fire brigade were powerless; nothing could go near such an inferno. There was nothing to be done but let the fire exhaust itself.

If this was true, it involved the loss of the Post Office Accountant's Office opposite the G.P.O., the Sackville Street Club, Gresham and Imperial Hotels, and other important buildings, and would have increased H.'s difficulties enormously, as it would have been necessary to build up the Post Office organisation again, with no records, registers, accounts, or documents of any kind – at best a stupendous task. However, fortunately this morning we hear the reports were exaggerated. The Imperial Hotel, Clery's great shop, and one or two others were burnt, but the upper part of the street escaped, and the Accountant's Office and the Sackville Street Club were not touched.

This morning Mr. C[oonan]., who has been H.'s great support all through this trying time (his second in command being away ill), and several other members of the staff are coming here, and with H. they are going down to see what remains of the G.P.O. It is being guarded from looters, as, from the enormous number of telegraph instruments destroyed, there must be a large quantity of copper and other metal, – a very valuable asset, – and also several thousand pounds in cash for payment of staff and soldiers' dependants, besides heaps of other valuable property.

Here I must tell you how absolutely heroic the telephone staff have been at the Exchange. It is in a building a considerable distance from the G.P.O., and the Sinn Feiners have made great efforts to capture it. The girls have been surrounded by firing; shots have several times come into the switch-room, where the men took down the boards from the back of the switch-boards and arranged them as shelters over the girls' heads to protect them from bullets and broken glass. Eight snipers have been shot on buildings commanding the Exchange, and one of the guard was killed yesterday; and these twenty girls have never failed. They have been on duty since Tuesday, sleeping when possible in a cellar and with indifferent food, and have cheerfully and devotedly stuck to their post, doing the work of forty. Only those on duty on the outbreak of the rebellion could remain; those in their homes could never get back, so with the aid of the men who take the night duty these girls have kept the whole service going. All telegrams have had to be sent by 'phone as far as the railway termini, and they have simply saved the situation. It has been magnificent!

The shooting is by no means over, as many of the Sinn Fein strongholds refuse to surrender. Jacob's biscuit factory is very strongly held, and when the rebels were called on to surrender they refused unless they were allowed to march out carrying their arms!

It is said that when Jacob was told that the military might have to blow up the factory he replied: "They may blow it to blazes for all I care; I shall never make another biscuit in Ireland." I don't know if this is true, but it very well may be, for he has been one of the model employers in Dublin, and almost gave up the factory at the time of the Larkin strike,

---

*As the book passes through the press, I learn on the one unimpeachable authority that the story about Messrs. Jacob & Co., however picturesque, is purely apocryphal. M.L.N.

and only continued it for the sake of his people; and so it will be with the few great industries in the city. Dublin is ruined.*

Yesterday I made a joyful discovery. When we came back from Italy in March, H. brought back from the office my large despatch-case in which I keep all F.'s letters. I did not remember what else was in it, so I investigated and found my necklet with jewelled cross and the pink topaz set (both of these being in large cases would not go in the jewel-case), also the large old paste buckle; so I am not absolutely destitute of jewellery. But, best of all, there were the three little handkerchiefs F. sent me from Armentières with my initial worked on them; for these I was grieving more than for anything, and when I found them the relief was so great I sat with them in my hand and cried.

This week has been a wonderful week for N. Never before has a boy of just seventeen had such an experience. Yesterday morning he was at the Automobile Club filling cans of petrol from casks for the Red Cross ambulance. He came in to lunch reeking of petrol. In the afternoon he went round with the Lord Mayor in an ambulance collecting food for forty starving refugees from the burnt-out district housed in the Mansion House, and after tea went out for wounded and brought in an old man of seventy-eight shot through the body. He was quite cheery over it, and asked N. if he thought he would recover. "Good Lord! yes; why not?" said N., and bucked the old man up!

Some of the staff who came here this morning had seen a copy of the *Daily Mail* yesterday, which devoted about six lines to the condition of things in Ireland and spoke of a Sinn Fein riot in which four soldiers and about six rebels had been killed. If that is all the English people are being told of a rebellion which 30,000 troops and many batteries of artillery are engaged in putting down, my letter will be rather a surprise to you; and as the news must come out, the English people will hardly be pleased at being kept in the dark. Such

*This was exaggerated, our total casualties being about 1,380.

a rebellion cannot be suppressed like a Zeppelin raid. During the first three days our casualties were nearly 1,000; now we hear they are close on 2,000.*

The College of Surgeons in St. Stephen's Green is still held by the rebels, so the firing of machine-guns from the Shelbourne Hotel and the United Service Club goes on as before, and there is intermittent firing in all directions. I doubt if it will quite cease for some days, as these strongholds will not surrender. Also the incendiary fires will probably continue. The great fire in Sackville Street last night was no doubt the work of incendiaries, as all the fires had died down. There was no wind, no shells were being fired, and no reason for the outbreak, but with all the relations and sympathisers of the rebels at large the fires may very well continue.

The staff have just returned. They are quite unnerved by what they have seen; they report nothing left of the G.P.O. but the four outside walls and portico, so we have lost everything. They say it is like a burned city in France.

May 1st, 11 a.m.

I had no time to continue this yesterday, but during the afternoon three of the rebel strongholds surrendered – Jacob's, Boland's, and the College of Surgeons on St. Stephen's Green. From this last building 160 men surrendered and were marched down Grafton Street. It is said that among them was Countess Markievicz, dressed in a man's uniform. It is also said that the military made her take down the green republican flag flying over the building herself and replace it by a white one: when she surrendered she took off her bandolier and kissed it and her revolver before handing them, to the officer. She has been one of the most dangerous of the leaders, and I hope will be treated with the same severity as the men. People who saw them marched down Grafton Street said they held themselves erect, and looked absolutely defiant!

2 p.m.

To-day for the first time since Easter Monday the *Irish Times* issued a paper with news of the rebellion. Very pluckily they had brought out a paper on Tuesday, but it contained only the proclamation and no reference to the rebellion, but a long account of Gilbert and Sullivan's operas which were to have been performed this week.

To-day's paper bears the dates "Friday, Saturday, and Monday, April 28th, 29th, and May 1st" – an incident unique, I should think, in the history of the paper.

It contains the various proclamations in full, which I will cut out and send to you. Please keep them, as they will be of interest in the future.

The paper states that Sir R. Casement is a prisoner in the Tower. So he was not shot without trial, as we were told. It also gives a list of the large shops and business establishments that have been destroyed – a total of 146.

It really seemed delightful to hear the little paper boys calling their papers about the streets again, and they had a ready sale for their papers at three times their value. This so encouraged them that in the afternoon they were running about again calling "Stop press." Several people went out and bought papers, only to find they were the same papers they had paid 3*d.* for in the morning.

"But this is the same paper I bought this morning."

"Sure, and it is, ma'am, but there's been a power of these papers printed, and they're not going to print any more till they're all sold."

Another lady thought she would drive a lesson home, so she said: "But you said it was a 'Stop press', and you knew it was not."

"It is, miss, but sure they hadn't time to print the 'stop

Inside the General Post Office in the aftermath of the Rising (Valentine Collection) Courtesy of the National Library of Ireland

Countess Markievicz (Keogh Collection) Courtesy of the National Library of Ireland

Royal College of Surgeons (Lawrence Collection) Courtesy of the National
Library of Ireland

The Shelbourne Hotel from St. Stephen's Green (Lawrence Collection) Courtesy
of the National Library of Ireland

View of Royal Hibernian Hotel from Molesworth Street, 1946 (Hope Collection)
Courtesy of the National Library of Ireland

press' on it!!"

("Stop press" is the latest news, usually printed on the back of the paper.)

Anyway, so great was the relief at seeing a paper again that no one grudged the urchins their little harvest.

Yesterday H. visited the Telephone Exchange, and a point was cleared up that has mystified everyone; and that is why, when the rebels on Easter Monday took every building of importance and every strategic position, did they overlook the Telephone Exchange? Had they taken it we should have been absolutely powerless, unable to send messages or telegrams for troops. The exchange is situated in Crown Alley, off Dame Street, and the superintendent told H. an extraordinary story. It seems when the rebels had taken the G.P.O. they marched a detachment to take the exchange, when just as they were turning into Crown Alley an old woman rushed towards them with arms held up calling out, "Go back, boys, go back; the place is crammed with military"; and supposing it to be in the hands of our troops they turned back. This was at noon. At 5 p.m. our troops arrived and took it over.

This saved the whole situation. Whether the woman was on our side or whether she thought she had seen soldiers will never be known.

When at the Castle yesterday H. got a copy of *The Times* for Saturday, the first paper we have seen since Monday, so you can imagine how eagerly we scanned the news about Ireland. More has got out than we expected, but still nothing like the true position. We rubbed our eyes when we read that "two battalions" had been sent to Ireland, and wondered if it could possibly have been a printer's error for two divisions (40,000 men) which actually arrived on Wednesday. The people were in the streets of Kingstown for twenty hours watching the troops pass through. Since then many more troops and artillery have come in.

2 p.m.

I have just returned from walking round the G.P.O. and Sackville Street with H. and some of the officials. It passes all my powers of description, only one word describes it, "Desolation." If you look at pictures of Yprès or Louvain after the bombardment it will give you some idea of the scene.

We looked up through the windows of the G.P.O. and saw the safe that was in H.'s room still in the wall, and the door does not appear to have been opened or the safe touched, but the whole place has been such an inferno one would think the door must have been red-hot. Among all the *débris* the fire was still smouldering, and we could not penetrate inside. I picked up a great lump of molten metal, a fantastic shape with bits of glass embedded in it. It is bright like silver, but they tell me it is lead. It is quite curious. Do you realise, G., that out of all H.'s library he now does not possess a single book, except one volume of his Dante, and I not even a silver teaspoon!!

Everything belonging to F. has gone; as he gave his life in the war, so an act of war has robbed us of everything belonging to him – our most precious possession.

It has almost broken H. up; but he has no time to think, which is perhaps a good thing.

The old Morland and Smith mezzotints have also gone – things we can never replace.

Behind the G.P.O. was the Coliseum Theatre, now only a shell; and on the other side of the street was the office of the *Freeman's Journal,* with all the printing machinery lying among the *débris,* all twisted and distorted; but, worst of all, behind that was a great riding school, where all the horses were burnt to death.

If at all possible you ought to come over for Whitsuntide. You will see such a sight as you will never see in your life unless you go to Belgium.

When we came here H. was scandalised at the condition of the G.P.O. The whole frontage was given up to sorting offices, and the public office was in a side street, a miserable, dirty little place, that would have been a disgrace to a small country town.

H. found that plans had been drawn up and passed for the complete reconstruction of the interior, building in a portion of the courtyard an office for sorting purposes, leaving the frontage for the public office with entrance under the great portico.

So H. *hustled,* and the work was completed and opened to the public six weeks ago.

It was really beautiful. The roof was a large glass dome, with elaborate plaster work, beautiful white pillars, mosaic floor, counters all of red teak wood, and bright brass fittings everywhere – a public building of which any great city might be proud; and in six weeks all that is left is a smoking heap of ashes!

N. had an extraordinary find inside one of the rooms. About six yards from the main wall he found, covered with ashes and a beam lying across it, a motor cycle. It was lying on its side. He got it out and found it perfect, tyres uninjured and petrol in the tank, and he rode it to the hotel, and has now taken it to the Castle to hand over to the police.

May 2nd, 10 *a.m.*

Last evening after tea I walked all round the ruined district with N. and two ladies from the hotel. The streets were thronged with people, and threading their way among the crowd were all sorts of vehicles: carts carrying the bodies of dead horses that had been shot the first day and lain in the streets ever since; fire brigade ambulances, followed by Irish cars bringing priests and driven by fire brigade men. Then motors with Red Cross emblems carrying white-jacketed doctors would dart along, followed by a trail of Red Cross nurses on bicycles, in their print dresses and white overalls, their white cap-ends floating behind them, all speeding on their errand of mercy to the stricken city.

From time to time we came across on the unwashed pavement the large dark stain telling its own grim story, and in one place the blood had flowed along the pavement for some yards and down into the gutter; but enough of horrors. We came sadly back, and on the steps we met Mr. O'B. returning from a similar walk. He could hardly speak of it, and said he stood in Sackville Street and cried, and many other men did the same.

Last night after dinner we were sitting in the room H. uses as a temporary office overlooking the street, when firing began just outside. They were evidently firing at the offices of the Sinn Fein Volunteers at the bottom of the road. It was probably the last stand of the rebels, and the firing was very sharp and quick. We thought bullets must come into the hotel. I was reading aloud some bits out of the *Daily Mail*, and the men were smoking. They moved my chair back to the wall between the windows out of the line of fire; but the firing became so violent we decided it was foolhardy to remain, so we deserted the room, took our papers, and went and sat on the stairs till it was over.

Since then we have not heard a shot fired; and it would seem that as we were present at the first shots fired in Sackville Street on Easter Monday so we have been present at the last fired eight days later in Dawson Street.

Out of all the novel experiences of the last eight days two things strike me very forcibly. The first is that, under circumstances that might well have tried the nerves of the strongest, there has been no trace of fear or panic among the people in the hotel, either among the guests or staff. Anxiety for absent friends of whom no tidings could be heard, though living only in the next square, one both felt and heard; but of fear for their own personal safety I have seen not one trace, and the noise of battle after the first two days seemed to produce nothing but boredom. The other is a total absence of thankfulness at our own escape.

It may come; I don't know. Others may feel it; I don't. I don't pretend to understand it; but so it is. Life as it has been lived for the last two years in the midst of death seems to have blunted one's desire for it, and completely changed one's feelings towards the Hereafter.

Now, G., I will end this long letter, and my next will probably deal with normal if less interesting matters, but intense interest must remain in the reconstruction of this great city.

Surely it must be possible to find men who will rule with firmness and understanding this fine people – so kindly, so emotional, so clever, so easily guided, and so magnificent when wisely led. One prays they may be found, and found quickly, and that we may live to see a Dublin restored to its former stateliness with a Government worthy of the nation.

Ever yours,

L. N.

FOURTH LETTER

Thursday, May 4th

DEAREST G., – I had not intended writing again so soon, but things are still happening that I think you will like to know, so I am going on with this series of letters, though I don't know when you will get them. But as by this time you will have seen N. you will have heard many details from him. How much he will have to tell his school-fellows when he returns to Shrewsbury to-morrow! I hoped to have sent my second and third letters by N., and in fact had actually packed them with his things. But when I told H. he said the rules were so stringent about letters that N. would certainly be questioned as to whether he was carrying any, and if he replied in the affirmative, which he certainly would have done, the letters would undoubtedly be confiscated and N. might get into serious trouble. So I had to unpack them again and must keep them till the censorship is removed, which will probably be in a few days. They have been written under much stress of circumstances, and are the only record we have of this most deeply interesting time, so I don't want to lose them altogether.

I am not too well, as they say here. The loss of eight nights' sleep seems to have robbed me of the power of sleeping for more than an hour or two at a stretch, and even that is attended often with horrid dreams and nightmares. But this is only the effect of over-strain, and no doubt will pass, though my head feels like a feather bed; so don't expect too much from these later letters.

Last night after dinner, when H. and I were sitting upstairs in attendance on the telephone, who should walk in but Dr. W. We had not met throughout the rebellion, so he had heaps to tell us. His wife and children were down at Greystones, and the poor thing had had a terribly anxious time, hearing nothing reliable of her husband or of her father, Lord S. What she did hear was that Dr. W. had been killed and also that H. had been shot in the G.P.O. She became so anxious that her faithful Scotch nurse was determined to get into Dublin and get news or die in the attempt. I must tell you her adventures, not only to show you how impossible it was to get into the city, but also it is such an extraordinary story of endurance and devotion that it ought to be recorded.

The girl started from Greystones at 2.30 p.m. on the Thursday, I think it was, carrying for the officers' home 14 lbs. of beef and 4 lbs. of butter, as Mrs. W. feared supplies would have run short, since nothing could be got in Dublin except at exorbitant prices (7s. a dozen for eggs and 14s. for a pair of chickens); so the girl started carrying a dead weight of 18 lbs.

She walked to Bray (five miles) and took train to Kingstown; here she had to take to the road, as the line beyond Kingstown was wrecked. She walked to Merrion Gates along the tram line about four miles, when she was stopped by sentries. She retraced her steps as far as Merrion Avenue (one mile), went up Merrion Avenue, and tried the Stillorgan–Donnybrook route. Here she got as far as Leeson Street Bridge (six miles), when she was within 800 yards of her destination, Dr. W.'s house. Here again she was stopped by sentries and turned back. She walked back to Blackrock (seven miles), when she was again stopped by sentries. She then returned up Merrion Avenue and, seeing that all routes were impossible to Dublin, took the road to Killiney (five miles), where she arrived about 11.30 p.m., having done thirty miles. Here she got hospitality at a cottage and stayed the remainder of the night there, paying for her accommodation with the 4 lbs. of butter, but she stuck gamely to the beef.

Next day she walked five miles to Shankhill, when she met a cart going to Bray *viâ* Killiney, so she rode back to Killiney on it and from thence to Bray. She then walked the five miles from Bray back to Greystones, her starting point.

Arrived back, she reached home absolutely exhausted, having walked forty miles, and dropped down saying, "There's your beef, and I never got there or heard anything." Mrs. W. was greatly distressed at her having carried the meat back when so exhausted and asked her why she had not given it away. "And what for should I give it away when we'll be wanting it ourselves maybe?"

Next day Dr. W. managed to get a telephone message through to his wife and relieved her anxiety.

He told us that on the first or second night of the rebellion – he could not remember which – two ladies of the Vigilance

71

Committee patrolling the streets at night came on a soldier lying wounded in an alley off Dawson Street, where he had crawled on being wounded. They went to Mercer's Hospital and gave information, and stretcher-bearers were sent out to bring in the man, the ladies accompanying them. When he was on the stretcher the two ladies walked up to the railings of St. Stephen's Green and gave the Sinn Feiners inside a regular dressing down, telling them they were skunks and cowards to shoot people down from behind bushes and asking them why they did not come out and fight in the open like men. Meanwhile the stretcher-bearers had taken the man to the hospital, where Dr. W. saw him.

"Well, my man; where are you hurt?"

"Divil a pellet, sorr, above the knee," laughing.

"Does it pain you?"

Not at all, sorr. Wait till I show you." He pulled up his trousers and showed five bullet shots below the knee.

"What regiment?"

"Royal Irish, sorr, like Michael Cassidy, of Irish nationality; and I bear no ill-will to nobody."

Cheery soul! His great pride was that about forty shots had been fired at him and not one hit him above the knee.

Dr. W. must bear a charmed life. He told us of several escapes he had. One, the most dramatic, I must tell you.

You know he is one of the surgeons to Mercer's Hospital, and had to be perpetually operating there at all hours of the day and night, besides having his own private hospital, in which he takes wounded officers. It too was filled with rebellion victims, so his work was tremendous.

One night he left Mercer's about 1 a.m., accompanied by another doctor. When passing in front of the Shelbourne Hotel they were challenged by our troops there. On explaining who they were they were of course allowed to proceed, and they stepped briskly out, wanting to get home. Suddenly, on the same pavement, about twenty yards away as far as they could judge in the black darkness, out flashed

two little lights from small electric lamps, evidently Sinn Fein signals. Dr. W. stopped and said to his companion: "Did you see that? it was a signal," when almost before the words were out of his mouth two rifles blazed straight at them, almost blinding them with the flash, and they *felt* the bullets whiz past their heads. The two Sinn Feiners, having signalled, waited long enough to see if their signal was returned, and then fired straight at where by their footsteps they supposed Dr. W. and his friend to be, and missed them by an inch or two.

Dr. W. and his friend got into the shelter of a doorway and flattened themselves out, trying to look as if they were not there, and quite forgetting that they both had lighted cigarettes, whose red tips should have been a beacon light to a vital spot had the Sinn Feiners noticed them. But for some reason they did not proceed further, and Dr. W. heard their steps dying away in the distance. Meanwhile his companion had his finger on the electric bell of the doorway where they were hiding, and after a time which seemed like an eternity an upper window opened and a voice inquired who was there, whereupon the woman of the house came down and let them in, and they spent the remainder of the night there.

Yesterday the Post Office was able to pay the separation allowances to the soldiers' wives. Last week of course it was impossible, but as it would have been equally impossible for them to have bought anything it did not so much matter. The question was how to get so large a sum of money round to the outlying post offices in safety, for, though the city is now comparatively safe, there are still snipers in outlying districts, and any party of Post Office officials known to have possession of large sums of money would undoubtedly have been attacked. So H. bethought him to requisition for one of the boiler armoured cars with military guard, and it was at once granted him. We had heard of them from N., but had not seen one, and great was the excitement at the hotel when this huge monster arrived for H.'s instructions. We all went out and examined it.

It was not one of Guinness's, but one that had been rigged up by one of the railway companies, with an engine boiler fixed on to a huge motor trolley, all painted light grey; and all down each side were black dots in an elegant design-something like this:-

Here and there one of these squares was cut out and acted as an air-hole, but they all looked exactly alike, so a sniper on a roof or from a window aiming at one of these squares probably found his bullet struck iron and bounded off to the accompaniment of derisive jeers from the "Tommies" inside. From the hotel the car proceeded to the Bank of Ireland, and took over £10,000 in *silver,* and started on its round to all the post offices, delivering the money in perfect safety. I will try and send you a photograph of one of these most ingenious conveyances.

After it had started on its round I went with H. to see the temporary sorting offices. H. had secured an enormous skating rink at the back of the Rotunda, and here all the sorting of letters was going on, with no apparatus whatever except what the men had contrived for themselves out of seats, benches and old scenery. They were all hard at work – a regular hive of bees. We think it is greatly to the credit of the Post Office staff that in twelve days from the *outbreak* of the rebellion and three days after the actual cessation of hostilities the whole service was reorganised, with two deliveries a day in Dublin, besides the ordinary country and mail deliveries. The engineers and telegraphists were no less wonderful. Indeed the staff from top to bottom of the office have worked splendidly, and H. is very proud of them. We

Armoured car

looked in at the poor G.P.O. on our way back. It is still smouldering, and it will be quite a fortnight before any excavations can be begun, but H. hopes to get the safe that contains many of our treasures out of the wall and opened in a few days.

To-day a Dr. C. who is staying in the hotel told me of an extraordinary escape he had had during one of the days of the rebellion. He was walking through one of the squares, which he had been told was clear of snipers, with an old friend of about eighty, when suddenly a bullet struck the pavement at the feet of his friend and ricochetted off. It was within an inch of the old gentleman's feet, and he was greatly interested, wanting to find the bullet to keep as a memento. While they were looking about for it a man who had been walking just behind them passed them on the pavement, and had only gone a few yards when they heard a second rifle shot, and the man dropped like a stone, shot through the heart. Dr. C. ran up to him, but he was quite dead. There was absolutely no safety anywhere from the snipers; man, woman, or child, nothing came amiss to them. It was dastardly fighting, if it could be called fighting at all.

A few days after St. Stephen's Green was supposed to have been cleared of rebels, we were told of a young woman whose husband was home from the war wounded and in one of the hospitals. She was going to see him, so took a short cut through the Green, when she was shot through the thigh; it is supposed by a rebel, in hiding in the shrubberies.

Sunday, 7th

I am sending off my other letters to you to-morrow, as we hear the censorship is no longer so strict, and as from the papers the position here seems now to be known in England private letters are not likely to be stopped. I will keep this till the safe is opened and tell you the result.

15th

To-day Mr. O'B. brought his wife to see me, and they have offered us their lovely house, Celbridge Abbey, about ten miles from Dublin, for five or six weeks from June 1st as they are going abroad again, and they thought we should like it for a change. We are more than grateful, as all our plans for going to Greystones for June and July are knocked on the head; but to Celbridge there is a good train service, and H. can come into Dublin every day, while I can revel in the lovely garden and grounds and recover in the peace and quiet my lost powers of sleep. What a kind thought it is, and how welcome at such a time! Celbridge Abbey was the home of Swift's "Vanessa", and later of Grattan, Ireland's greatest orator, so is a most interesting and historical place.

17 *th*

To-day the safe was opened, and contained nothing of any value, only a few official papers!

With this has gone our last hope of any salvage from the wreck of our property. Dillon's "perfect gentlemen," of whom he expressed himself so proud in the House the other night, had evidently broken open H.'s great official desk, and found the key of the safe and abstracted my jewel-case, F.'s field-glasses and several other of his much-prized possessions, and then locked the safe again. The only document they stole from among the official documents was F.'s commission. Why, we cannot imagine, unless the fact that it bore the King's signature made it worthy of special insult and desecration.

H. was very sad when he told me, but I think I am past caring about any possessions now. F. and all his precious things are gone. Nothing else seems worth considering. Perhaps some day we may pluck up heart to collect things again around us, but at present one can only feel, "Let the dead bury the dead."

20 *th*

To-day they are beginning on the excavations of H.'s room; the fire burnt with such ferocity that there is much less rubble in it than one would imagine. As you probably remember, H.'s room was on the first floor, with a storey above it. When the whole place fell in, H.'s room fell through into the room below, and a portion of that had fallen through to the cellars. The men are removing everything of the nature of bricks and iron and stone coping of the roof, and then four extra-careful men are to be put on to shovel up the rest of the *débris,* which is burnt to powder, and Noblett, H.'s confidential messenger, is going to be there to receive anything of ours that may be found.

23rd

Yesterday morning and this morning I have been down watching the excavations of H.'s room. It is quite like the excavations at Pompeii. Every shovelful is most carefully overlooked, and several of our things have turned up, though so far nothing of any intrinsic value. When I went there yesterday morning Noblett produced a great lump of molten glass of no shape or form with one or two metal nobs sticking up at odd angles. He thought it was the remains of a cruet, but we had none; and on further examination it flashed across my mind that it was the cut-glass bottles in the large rosewood and brass-bound dressing-case in which I had packed all my jewellery – family miniatures, four gold watches and chains; diamond pendant, etc. It had been stolen out of the safe, and evidently the looters had not been able to get it away. Noblett was thrilled, and the men redoubled their carefulness, hoping to find some of the jewellery. When I went down again in the afternoon Noblett produced three little brooches that F. had given me on various birthdays when a wee boy. He always went out with his own sixpence, and nearly always returned with a brooch, which I used to wear with great pride. One, a Swastika brooch, he gave me when he was at Margate after that terrible illness, and he used to go on the pier in his bath-chair. The blue enamel on it was intact in several places; the other two were intact in form, but charred and black, with the pins burnt off. But how glad I was to see them again! During the afternoon two or three more brooches turned up, but nothing of any value whatever. So we came to the conclusion the rebels had broken open the box and taken out everything of value and thrown away the rest. The few burnt bits of jewellery that were found all came from one spot.

This morning when I went Noblett had nearly a sackful of curiosities, which I sorted over. Evidently these were the whole contents of the canteen of plated things we used to take with us when we took a furnished house and put the silver in a bank, quantities of spoons and forks, black, and looking like old iron, many twisted into weird shapes, and the knives, which were new when we came here, without a scrap of ivory handle, and the blades burnt and twisted in the most extraordinary way. A most miserable-looking collection, fit only for the dust-heap.

25*th*

They are nearing the end of the excavations, and nothing of any value has been found. This morning when I went I found them cutting into a mound of what looked like solid white chalk. I could not imagine what it could be, but the men told me it was the books that had been stored in one of the great mahogany presses; not a trace of burnt wood was found. I could not believe that books could be reduced to such a substance. I had expected to find quantities of charred black paper, with possibly some fragments of binding, and was quite incredulous. However, on examining it I found the substance was in layers like the leaves of a book, but when I picked some up it felt like silk between my fingers, and you could blow it away like thistle-down. Had I not seen it myself I should never have believed such a thing possible. Besides H.'s and F.'s books there were a number of great official books in leather bindings half an inch thick, but all was reduced to the same substance.

Noblett gave me to-day one of Princess Mary's gift boxes that had been sent to me by a soldier at the front; except for being black instead of bright brass, it was absolutely uninjured – the medallion in the centre, and the inscription, date, etc., perfect. The Christmas card inside and the Queen's letter were just black charred paper, but you could see the M. and the crown above it on the card. Also an antique brass snuff-box inlaid with mother-of-pearl turned up but little injured.

26*th*

To-day the men finished their work on H.'s room. At the last about eight fragments of silver forks and two tablespoons were taken out and a foot of a silver sugar-bowl with a bit of something that looked like burnt tissue paper attached to it; and that was all that was found of all our silver. The half of a copper base of one of our beautiful Sheffield plate candelabra came out of one of the last shovelfuls, – and there was an end of all our property.

So that page is turned, and it seems a good place to end this over-long letter. On Thursday we go down to Celbridge, where with memories of Swift and the wretched and foolish Vanessa and in company with a beautiful swan and swaness, which bring their babies to the lawn to be admired and duly fed, I am going to rest and recuperate for the next five weeks and try to remember out of this awful time only the kindness and sympathy that has been shown to us by so many Irish friends. I shall not write any more of these diary letters unless there are further acute developments, which God forbid.

Ever yours,

L. N.

PROCLAMATION DECLARING MARTIAL LAW

WHEREAS, in different parts of Ireland certain evilly disposed persons and associations, with the intent to subvert the Supremacy of the Crown in Ireland, have committed divers acts of violence, and have with deadly weapons attacked the Forces of the Crown, and have resisted by armed forces the lawful authority of His Majesty's Police and Military Forces:

And, WHEREAS, by reason thereof, several of His Majesty's liege subjects have been killed, and many others severely injured, and much damage to property has been caused:

And, WHEREAS, such armed resistance to His Majesty's authority still continues,

Now I, IVOR CHURCHILL BARON WIMBORNE, Lord Lieutenant General and General Governor of Ireland, by virtue of all the powers thereunto me enabling,

Do HEREBY PROCLAIM that, from and after the date of this Proclamation, and for the period of one month thereafter (unless otherwise ordered), that part of the United Kingdom called Ireland is under and subject to Martial Law.

AND I DO HEREBY call on all loyal and well-affected subjects of the Crown to aid in upholding and maintaining the peace of this Realm and the Supremacy and authority of the Crown, and to obey and conform to all Orders and Regulations of the Military Authority. And I warn all peaceable and law-abiding subjects in Ireland of the danger of frequenting, or being in, any place in or in the vicinity of which His Majesty's Forces are engaged in the suppression of disorder.

AND I DO DECLARE that all persons found carrying arms, without lawful authority, are liable to be dealt with by virtue of this Proclamation.

GIVEN AT DUBLIN
This 29th Day of April 1916.
(Signed) WIMBORNE.
GOD SAVE THE KING.

The Sinn Féin Rebellion

PROCLAMATION POSTED OUTSIDE
THE GENERAL POST OFFICE.

POBLAGHT NA H EIREANN

The Provisional Government
of the
IRISH REPUBLIC

To the People of Ireland.

IRISHMEN AND IRISHWOMEN: In the name of God and of the dead generations from which she receives her old tradition of Nationhood, IRELAND, through us, summons her Children to her flag and strikes for her freedom.

Having organised and trained her manhood through her secret revolutionary organisation, the Irish Republican Brotherhood, and through her open military organisations, the Irish Volunteers and the Irish Citizen Army, having patiently perfected her discipline, having resolutely waited for the right moment to reveal itself, she now seizes that moment, and, supported by her exiled Children in America and by gallant Allies in Europe, but relying in the first on her own strength, she strikes in full confidence of victory.

WE DECLARE the right of the people of Ireland to the ownership of Ireland, and to the unfettered control of Irish destinies, to be sovereign and indefeasible. The long usurpation of that right by a foreign people and Government has not extinguished the right, nor can it ever be extinguished except by the destruction of the Irish people. In every generation the Irish people have asserted their right to national freedom and sovereignty; six times during the past three hundred years they have asserted it in arms. Standing on that fundamental right and again asserting it in arms in the face of the world, we hereby proclaim the Irish Republic as a Sovereign Independent State, and we pledge our lives and the lives of our comrades-in-arms to the cause of its freedom, of its welfare, and of its exaltation among the nations.

THE IRISH REPUBLIC is entitled to, and HEREBY CLAIMS, the allegiance of every Irishman and Irishwoman. The Republic guarantees religious and civil liberty, equal rights and equal opportunities to all its citizens, and declares its resolve to pursue the happiness and prosperity of the whole

82

nation and of all its parts, cherishing all the children of the Nation equally, and oblivious of the differences carefully fostered by an Alien Government, which have divided a minority from the majority in the past.

Until our arms have brought the opportune moment for the establishment of a permanent National Government, representative of the whole people of Ireland and elected by the suffrages of all her men and women, the Provisional Government, hereby constituted, will administer the civil and military affairs of the Republic in trust for the people.

We place the cause of the Irish Republic under the protection of the Most High God, Whose blessing we invoke upon our arms, and we pray that no one who serves that cause will dishonour it by cowardice, inhumanity, or rapine. In this supreme hour the Irish Nation must, by its valour and discipline and by the readiness of its children to sacrifice themselves for the common good, prove itself worthy of the august destiny to which it is called.

Signed on behalf of the Provisional Government,

THOMAS CLARKE.

SEAN MACDIARMADA.	THOMAS MACDONAGH.
P. H. PEARSE.	EAMONN CEANNT.
JAMES CONNOLLY.	JOSEPH PLUNKETT.

MANIFESTO ISSUED FROM THE REBEL HEADQUARTERS, GENERAL POST OFFICE.

HEADQUARTERS ARMY OF THE IRISH REPUBLIC.
General Post Office, Dublin.
28th April 1916 – 9.30 a.m.

The Forces of the Irish Republic, which was proclaimed in Dublin on Easter Monday 24th April, have been in possession of the central part of the Capital since 12 noon on that day. Up to yesterday afternoon Headquarters was in touch with all the main outlying positions, and despite furious and almost continuous assaults by the British Forces all those positions were then still being held, and the Commandants in charge were confident of their ability to hold them for a long time.

During the course of yesterday afternoon and evening the enemy succeeded in cutting our communications with our other positions in the city, and Headquarters is to-day isolated.

The enemy has burnt down whole blocks of houses, apparently with the object of giving themselves a clear field for the play of artillery and field guns against us.

We have been bombarded during the evening and night by shrapnel and machine-gun fire, but without material damage to our position, which is of great strength.

We are busy completing arrangements for the final defence of Headquarters and are determined to hold it while the buildings last.

I desire now, lest I may not have an opportunity later; to pay homage to the gallantry of the soldiers of Irish Freedom who have during the past four days been writing with fire and steel the most glorious chapter in the later history of Ireland. Justice can never be done to their heroism, to their discipline, to their gay and unconquerable spirit in the midst of peril and death.

Let me, who have led them into this, speak in my own, and in my fellow Commanders' names, and in the name of Ireland present and to come, their praises, and ask those who come after them to remember them.

For four days they have fought and toiled, almost without cessation, almost without sleep; and in the intervals of fighting they have sung songs of the freedom of Ireland.

No man has complained, no man has asked "Why?" Each individual has spent himself, happy to pour out his strength for Ireland and for freedom. If they do not win this fight, they will at least have deserved to win it. But win it they will, although they may win it in death. Already they have won a great thing. They have redeemed Dublin from many shames, and made her name splendid among the names of cities.

If I were to mention names of individuals my list would be a long one. I will name only that of Commandant General James Connolly, commanding the Dublin division. He is wounded, but is still the guiding brain of our resistance.

If we accomplish no more than we have accomplished, I am satisfied. I am satisfied that we have saved Ireland's honour. I am satisfied that we should have accomplished more, that we should have accomplished the task of enthroning, as well as proclaiming the Irish Republic as a Sovereign State, had our arrangements for a simultaneous rising of the whole country, with a combined plan as sound as the Dublin plan has been proved to be, been allowed to go through on Easter Sunday. Of the fatal countermanding order which prevented those plans from being carried out, I shall not speak further. Both Eoin MacNeill and we have acted in the best interests of Ireland.

For my part, as to anything I have done in this, I am not afraid to face either the judgment of God, or the judgment of posterity.

(Signed) P. H. PEARSE,
Commandant General,
Commanding-in-Chief the Army of the Irish Republic and President of
the Provisional Government.

The day following this proclamation the rebels surrendered unconditionally.

Irish Experiences
in War

ARTHUR HAMILTON NORWAY

Irish Experiences
in War

It was suggested to me lately, by Sir Andrew Wingate,[1] that a certain public importance attaches to my experiences in Ireland as Secretary of the Post Office in that country, and that they are worth recording, not indeed as possessing consequence at all equal to that of the great and dangerous crises in which England was involved on the Continent of Europe, but rather as illustrating certain tendencies of Government which have, in other generations as well as ours, proved a weakness to our country, and permitted the growth of evils which might have been eradicated if recognised and faced at an early stage.

I have accepted this suggestion half unwillingly, because a doubt obtrudes itself whether I can tell the tale even now that more than ten years have passed, and I am far withdrawn from active life, without some strong feeling which might be inconsistent with the honest tradition of loyalty to their political heads in which British Civil Servants are trained and which becomes the habit of their life. But I do not write for publication. I have kept silence for many years, and if I break it now, it is only in my study, and for the information of my family, and especially of any coming after me who may care to ask themselves what I did in difficult circumstances. They are entitled to this knowledge, if they desire it. And if not, it is but to leave these pages unread or to put them in the fire.

In the year 1912 I was one of the Assistant Secretaries of the Post Office, having then spent rather less than thirty years on the highest grade of the Civil Service; and the Irish appointment was not one lying in my direct way. In fact, it was of rather lower standing, and of the same pay, namely £1,200 per annum, so that it could not be offered to me as a promotion. But my dear wife had been subjected to a severe operation, and had recently lost her mother, to whom she was deeply attached; so that I welcomed for her the opportunity of a change of scene. My son Fred, moreover, had had grave ill health at Rugby, and for him too I thought the change to Ireland would be advantageous. So I sought the appointment, and it could scarcely be refused to me, since my standing and influence in the service were high, and would have justified me in seeking any change of work which could be given to me reasonably. And so, after I had put aside various suggestions that I was imperilling my chances of the Second Secretaryship by going out of the line of promotion, the Postmaster General, Sir Herbert Samuel, appointed me, and I took up office in Dublin in September 1912.

The dominant question in Ireland at that time was Home Rule, and it may be well to say that the system of Government denoted by that phrase differed widely from the Dominion status which has now been conferred on Southern Ireland, since it proposed the creation of a purely subordinate legislature in Dublin, subject in all respects to the ultimate control of Parliament at Westminster, which could not only review all acts of the Irish Government, but could, if it thought right, reverse them, and give to the reverse statutes the force of law in Ireland. It is important to remember that this was the extreme length to which the Liberal Party, the only supporters of Home Rule in Great Britain, had ever proposed to go towards satisfying the insistent claims of Irish Nationalists. The idea of conceding Dominion status, or in any other way releasing the acts of an Irish Legislature from British control, was not part of the policy of any British party, and was indeed repudiated by all politicians of responsibility. I was myself a liberal of the imperialist school led by Lord Rosebery, and Sir Edward Grey; and relying on the maintenance of British control, I did not see real danger to the welfare of the British Empire in the concession of Home Rule of the type proposed.

Such however as it was, the proposal was resented fiercely by Conservatives in Great Britain and Ireland, and excited small enthusiasm among Irish Nationalists, who accepted it with the avowed intention of using it to gain more. When I reached Ireland, society was divided very sharply, and little intercourse existed between those who supported Home Rule and those who opposed it, the former indeed having few, if any, representatives above the salt socially, while bitterness between the two was so great that almost the first piece of advice given to me was in no case to engage a parlour maid who was a Roman Catholic, since any talk which touched on politics at the dinner table would be reported to the priests. That this belief was not groundless was demonstrated a little later when a heedless letter from a guest, containing some sharp strictures on Nationalist Roman Catholics, and left carelessly by me upon the desk in my study, was stolen by a cook dismissed for insolence, who quoted some of its phrases in a last interview with my wife, and who did in all probability endeavour to stir up mischief by using it in some of those subterranean ways which are common enough in Ireland. No mischief resulted, however, and we were always on good terms with the priests and nuns in our neighbourhood, as well, of course, as with our own Church.

Lord Aberdeen was Viceroy when I took up duty, a kindly and well meaning man, but dull, and by no means strong enough to deal with the difficult situation which was even then growing up. The Chief Secretary was Mr Birrell, a shrewd literary critic, but a negligent and undiscerning politician, who did not occupy his Lodge in the Phoenix Park, and visited Ireland rarely. The Under Secretary, whose duty it was to know the country accurately, and to probe its movements deeply, was Sir James Dougherty, a man of supine temperament and narrow, if capable, ideas, to whom one would not look for quick and resolute action on the sudden appearance of a public danger. The Inspector General of the Royal Irish Constabulary was Sir Neville Chamberlain, a distinguished soldier and perhaps alive to the growth of trouble which he did not check. The head of the Dublin Metropolitan Police, an unarmed force, was Sir John Ross of Bladensburg, of whom I think with constant admiration as a fine and resolute man, completely loyal to his subordinates at a time of grave difficulty, of which I will say more later. All these, with the certain exception of the last, were dominated by the strong conviction held by Mr Birrell, and adopted as a principle of action by the Ministry, that Ireland must be governed according to Irish ideas, by which doctrine they understood that all strong action must be foregone, and everything avoided which might conceivably create friction.

Now the truth about the Irish is that they appreciate strength, despise weakness, and desire to be governed firmly and justly. But this was never known at Westminster, and any efforts to assert it were turned down contemptuously. It was indeed a chief difficulty of the situation that Irish disloyalty was not taken seriously in London, where it was usual to speak of it with contempt as displaying the characteristics of comic opera. It is certainly strange that administrators who well remembered the Phoenix Park murders, and innumerable other crimes committed in the eighties, should have subsided to the easy optimism which had spread through all departments of the Government when I reached Ireland. Everyone believed that the point was off the Irish pikes, and the gunmen had forgotten how to shoot. This was partly true. But it was also true that dangerous men and organisations were stirring in their sleep, while those who should have watched them played golf and dined in peace.

Within a few days of reaching Dublin I called on Sir James Dougherty, the Under Secretary, at the Castle, and naturally asked him about the state of the country. He expressed no anxiety nor did he indicate any source of difficulty likely to present itself to me. He told me, however, that the term Sinn Fein denoted every shade of Nationalism, from innocent enthusiasts for Gaelic literature and Gaelic sports at one end to red-hot Fenians at the other; so that to call a man a Sinn Feiner established nothing about him, until one knew to which section of Sinn Fein he belonged. There was truth in this, as I found later. But it would have been expressed more accurately by saying that the Sinn Fein movement, innocent enough at the outset, had been adopted by dangerous men as a screen, much as they used the Gaelic Athletic Association somewhat later, or perhaps even then, making use of the organisation of both Societies to cloak their meetings, and professing, if questions arose, the simplest enthusiasm for Gaelic sport and literature. I do not know whether Sir James Dougherty suspected this. He certainly gave me no hint of it. I discovered the fact independently of him, and before dropping the point I may say that before the rebellion broke out the dangerous elements in Sinn Fein, no less than in the Gaelic Athletic Association, had eaten up the rest, and the whole of both was to be taken seriously, though wise men need not have feared them. This rather clever policy of screening was, I think, new in Ireland, and to some extent may excuse the singular failure to recognise the approach of danger.

It is scarcely worth while to speak of the attitude of Lord Aberdeen, for I can recall no observation of value which he ever made to me on the condition of the country, or any other matter. In all quarters I found the same light complacency. The country was quiet. Why should it not remain so? But ere long I began to get an occasional police report indicating that a member of my staff was suspected of belonging to the Irish Republican Brotherhood, of which I had not heard before. In my office there was none who could, or would, tell me the nature of the Brotherhood. So I pursued enquiries in the Sackville Street Club, of which I was a member, but at first with no better success, for men seemed disinclined to talk of the matter. At last I asked a Resident Magistrate, one O'Sullivan, whether he knew anything of the Brotherhood. He looked startled, and answered, 'Not now. Formerly of course I did.' 'And what was it, when you knew it?' I continued. 'A black murder Society,' he rapped out, 'and never anything else.' 'Does it exist now?' I went on. 'I hope to God it doesn't,' he replied. 'You would be alarmed?' 'Very much indeed,' he said. And the conversation ended with a promise that he would satisfy himself about the existence of the Brotherhood in his own district, and tell me the result on his next visit to Dublin.

A fortnight later he came up to me in the smoking room, and assured me that he found no trace of it in his neighbourhood. I told him of my police reports, and he became grave, and warned me that the reports were probably indications of coming trouble.

I was sufficiently impressed by this to resolve to satisfy myself whether all the police reports affecting my staff reached me, and on enquiry at the Castle I found that they did not. I saw Sir Neville Chamberlain and Sir John Ross, and with little difficulty arranged that every report affecting in any way a Post Office servant was to be sent to me confidentially. I received them and studied them carefully, drawing conclusions which might have been of use had I succeeded in gaining attention for them. But preconceived ideas were rooted too strongly to admit the recognition of fresh facts by the Irish Govt., or by the Postmaster General.

While this study occupied many weeks, during which I collected as much information as I could about tendencies shaping themselves in the country, difficulty began to present itself for me at Post Offices in the North, where a growing opposition to Home Rule among the people, loyalist as they claimed to be, threatened forgetfulness of public duty no less than in the rest of Ireland. It was evident, of course, that with politics, as such, I, the head of the Post Office, had nothing to do. My duty was to secure that the staff of the Post Office did their work efficiently and impartially, and I began to see that I should have trouble in effecting this, trouble too of a kind for which neither my experience, nor that of any other high officer of the Post Office had any precedent, for sedition in England is too rare to be regarded seriously. There was however beginning to emerge, both North and South, a conviction that loyalty to political ends must override all other loyalties, and among the rest of course loyalty to the Postmaster General. Now this would be serious at any time. But the administrative problem which it threatened to raise was increased enormously by the consideration that the latter loyalty might become ere long of vital consequence to the safety of the Empire. For Army headquarters was uneasy about risks of invasion long before August 1914, and a year before that the danger of war sent important officers to my room with maps to explain in confidence what line would be held if the danger broke. Clearly, all operations would be imperilled if there were not full confidence in the secrecy and honour of the Post Office staff. The same considerations applied of course to any outbreak of rebellion on either side. My problem began to grow acute.

Naturally, I consulted my Chiefs in London, but had in answer only a request for any practicable suggestion. I had but one, of the effectiveness of which I was not sure, but which seemed worth trying. It was to contradict by a public warning to the staff the growing idea, sedulously propagated by both sides, that their duty as Post Office servants might be subordinated to their political action. I drafted a short notice to this effect, and proposed to put it up in all offices, arguing that not only would it serve to remind men and women of their duty, but it would put a useful answer in the hands of weaklings who were puzzled by specious balancings of two loyalties, and who could point to the notice and say, 'No. There is what my employer expects of me.' I still think this notice might have done much to save the situation, for most men and women are honest at heart, and will respond to a clear call. But the call was not given, for the Postmaster General thought the notice provocative, and others in London condemned it as unnecessary. None of them indicated any other step which could be taken, and the situation continued to drift.

In fact the problem how to keep the growing sedition out of the Irish Post Offices, and secure or maintain the safety of the communications, did not seem in London to be a problem at all, for none there regarded the peace of the country as seriously threatened. I had myself no certain conviction on the subject, materials for judgment being scanty and not always reliable. But I was uneasy, and in particular I wanted more information about the Irish Republican Brotherhood The only chance of obtaining any was through the Irish Government and to Dublin Castle accordingly I went. I told the Under Secretary that I heard disquieting things about the Brotherhood, and referred in particular to the police reports. A memorandum was obtained from the secret Intelligence Department, and sent on to me. It was to the effect that the Brotherhood had been troublesome in former days, but had subsided much in consequence, and might be regarded as dormant, and in fact negligible, comprising in its membership perhaps a thousand persons in all parts of Ireland. Nothing was said about the aims of the organisation, nor any warning given of its dangerous character. I did not see that I could do more. I locked the memorandum in my safe. This was some months before the war. The exact date I forget.

I am not writing history in detail, and I need only say that as the outbreak of war approached the Ulster Unionists drew closer towards armed rebellion, and their unpunished creation of an armed force was imitated most unhappily by the institution of the Irish Volunteers on the Nationalist side. Stories of gun running were rife, and at last in July a cargo of rifles was landed at Howth, and brought by road towards Dublin. Nothing was known, of course, at the Castle almost at the moment of landing. Quick and resolute action was needed to prevent the rifles from reaching Dublin. The Under Secretary was, I think, in England. The Lord Chancellor hesitated and lost time. Mr Harrell, second in command to Sir John Ross at the Dublin Metropolitan police, and son of a former Under Secretary, summoned a company of the K.O.B.[2] from the Barracks, acting largely on his own responsibility. The act cost him dear. He got the rifles. But in return to Dublin the soldiers were mobbed by an ugly crowd, and stone throwing began, not without injury to the soldiers, who fired on the crowd, killing and wounding several. The panic was terrible, and the city filled itself with a fierce anger which did much to increase the danger of the situation. Politicians, both Nationalist and Liberal, whipped up the indignation. The fatal word 'provocative' was applied to Mr Harrell's resolute action, even by those whose experience should have shown them the acute risk of allowing the rifles to reach an already excited city. A Commission presided over by Lord Shaw of Dunfermline was appointed to investigate the occurrences of that unhappy morning, and to placate Irish opinion, which was done by dismissing Mr Harrell, notwithstanding the firm support of Sir John Ross, his chief, support which he renewed with great courage before Lord Hardinge's Commission,[3] which investigated the outbreak of the rebellion, and of which I shall speak later.

It could not be supposed that the passions on which these and other grave incidents were the indication or the cause would fail to sap the loyalty of some of the 17,000 men and women under my authority at Irish Post Offices. My anxieties for the safety of the communications in my charge were not relieved by the fact that none in London shared them. I could not but wonder at times whether the easy confidence shown

97

across the Channel were not the wiser attitude, and the consequent distrust of my own judgment did not make my position easier, though I do not see that it led me to omit any possible precaution. There was none with whom I could take counsel in Ireland, for all were extreme on one side or the other, so fiercely passionate in denouncing the motives and acts of those who disagreed with them that consultation darkened counsel, and I was driven back on my own imperfect opportunities of deducing the truth. There were those in Dublin who were fond of saying, – the 'Irish Times' was among them – that the Post Office was full of Sinn Feiners, and that no steps were taken to discourage their activities. But of these critics none even once approached me with their evidence. Nor do I even now see that facts were in my possession at that time which would have justified me in holding that membership of Sinn Fein created a danger to the State, or rendered an officer less competent to serve the Postmaster General efficiently. Certainly, neither of these points was ever urged by the Irish Government, in whose custody, and not in mine, lay the safety of the country.

While I was groping for a clear conception of my duty in this maze of uncertainties, the war broke, like a blaze of light, bringing out in sharp relief every risk which had occurred to me; and others which had not, all suddenly turned vital, and invested with reality. I had gone to London, after much hesitation, to attend a large farewell dinner to my old friend, Sir Alexander King, who was resigning the Secretaryship of the Post Office. I had scarcely reached London when the storm broke, and the precautionary stage was declared. I went at once to the Postmaster General, Mr Charles Hobhouse, who while agreeing that my presence was needed at my office, insisted that I should stay for the dinner. I did, and sat next to Sir Matthew Nathan, with whom, as Secretary of the Post Office, my relations had not been free from friction. We met that night with cordiality, and he told me that he was to be the new Under Secretary in Dublin. He was a man of charming manners, to dine with whom was a very agreeable experience, since he was a courteous and polished host and had the instinct for entertaining. But he was not discerning, nor resolute. 'What is the use,' he said to me once, 'of contending against the stream of tendency?' 'That is fatalism,' I said. 'No,' he answered, 'it is good sense.' And his conception of loyalty was not to tell his political chief when he thought him wrong, but to help him in his policy without remonstrance, – wherein, I think, he acted rather as becomes a soldier than a Civil Servant occupying an important post.

It would be idle to attempt to recapture the impressions under which official life went on at the outset of the war. Embarkation was going on secretly and swiftly at many points in Ireland, and as it was of great importance that details of the units embarking should not leak out, the question what dependence could be placed on the Post Office staff leapt into the front, that is in Ireland, though in London the same easy confidence reigned unbroken. At Army headquarters in Dublin it did not. The first Post Office servant to fall under their ban was Hegarty, Postmaster of Queenstown, at which port many secret things were happening. A high officer called on me to say that Hegarty must not remain at Queenstown, or indeed in Ireland. I asked why, seeing that his official reputation was high and he held the complete confidence of Sir Andrew Ogilvie,[4] and other old colleagues of mine in the Secretariat, where he had worked for years before going to Queenstown. The answer was guarded, but explicit in this point, that Hegarty was known to have been in very recent communication with the German Ambassador. This was not all, for much suspicion rested on him. But relations of any sort with the German Ambassador at that moment served to show unsuitability for control of the Queenstown Office in war; and after receiving my assurance that I would act at once, the officer left me, remarking casually that in war time proved traitors were shot.

I found great difficulty about this case in London where

Ogilvie, and others acquainted with Hegarty, were most indignant that any one could doubt his loyalty, and fought stoutly against my reports. But I carried my point. Hegarty was transferred at once to the Postmastership of Whitchurch in Shropshire, where he remained throughout the war, giving rise to no further official trouble. But I may say, if only to show how baseless was the confidence felt in him by Ogilvie and others, and how just the unproved suspicions of the military Intelligence, that Hegarty has now written a book, in which he reveals that fact that even when he was earning golden opinions in the Secretariat he was already not only a secret member of the Irish Republican Brotherhood, but one of its chief directors, & that he continued to direct it actively from Whitchurch. Of this I had not the least inkling.

The moment was so critical, and the military judgment so clear, that the case of Hegarty caused me little trouble. It was otherwise with the next which occurred almost simultaneously. The towns in Ireland were placarded with recruiting posters, and a sorter in the Waterford Post Office was arrested by soldiers in the act of tearing down one of these. The evidence was clear, and the disloyalty of the act especially disgraceful in a servant of the State. How the military authorities would have dealt with the prisoner I do not know. For he had scarcely been arrested when one Michael Murphy, Nationalist member for Tramore, went to General Friend, Commander in Chief in Ireland, and threatened him that if the man was punished recruiting in Waterford would stop at once. General Friend yielded, and released the man. At once he claimed to resume duty, and that was where I came in. For it was obvious that the man was disloyal, and that his restoration to duty unpunished would be of the worst example to the staff, some of whom were wavering, both at Waterford and elsewhere. I went to Army headquarters, where I was assured that the General regretted already that he had released the man, that he saw the danger of restoring him to duty, and wished that I could do any thing to keep him out. He could not, however, arrest the man again. I thereupon went to the Castle, where I saw Sir Matthew Nathan, and suggested to him that he, as head of the permanent staff of the Irish Government, could, under the Defence of the Realm Act, keep this disloyal man out of any Irish Post Office. He did not dispute that he could do so, but refused, on the mere ground that General Friend had released the man. I then, having failed to move the military or the Civil authority in Ireland, reported to the Postmaster General my anxieties about the staff, contending that as a purely postal question, within his sole responsibility, it was undesirable to replace this man on duty. Apparently, my fears were considered, for I had no decision for three weeks, after which I was instructed to replace the man on duty, paying his wages for the whole period of his absence. I fear this case did not go unnoted.

About this time I noted in the police reports more frequent references than before to the I.R.B., which seemed to be more widely active than before; and desiring to know whether the Castle was aware of any growth of this evil organisation, I asked for another memorandum. This was obtained, and was to the effect that the I.R.B. was not quite so dormant, nor quite so insignificant in numbers, as at the date of the former memorandum. But it might still be regarded as unimportant and giving rise to no anxiety. Such was the last advice, which I received from the Irish Government on this grave matter. And as a comment on it, I transcribe here a few clauses from the proclamation of the Irish Republic posted in Dublin at the outbreak scarce a year later.

'Irishmen and Irishwomen. In the name of God and of the dead generations from which she receives her old tradition of Nationhood, Ireland, through us, summons her children to her flag, and strikes for her freedom.

Having organised and trained her manhood through her secret revolutionary organisation, the Irish Republican Brotherhood ... and supported by gallant Allies in Europe, but relying in the first on her own strength, she strikes in full confidence of victory.'

Thus, the I.R.B. was at the heart of the matter, and the complacent assurances of the Castle were fatally wrong. A determined effort to stamp out this dangerous body, versed as it has always been in murder and intrigue, might have cost many lives but would have freed Ireland from a terror whence no good thing can come, and saved the British Government from a failure more disgraceful than can easily be found in its great history.

Nothing known to me, or I think to others, at the time suggested the great part of the Brotherhood in the conspiracy. But it was clear enough that some organisation was using terror as a weapon, and in illustration of this I may note the case of another Hegarty, brother of the Postmaster of Queenstown, who was a sorter in the Cork Post Office, but fell under the ban of the active military Intelligence, who applied to me for his removal from Cork. The evidence pointed clearly enough to association with dangerous and disloyal men, but established no fact which could be said to justify punishment. Thus the case could only be met by transfer to an equivalent position out of Ireland, and I notified to Hegarty that he must go and work in England for a time, retaining his pay, and receiving in addition a subsistence allowance of a guinea a week. He protested. 'For what am I being punished?' he asked. 'You are not being punished,' I replied. 'But of what am I suspected?' 'No charge is made against you,' I said: 'but the Postmaster General decides in his discretion, as your employer, to employ you out of Ireland for the present.' 'Then' said he, 'I refuse to leave Ireland.' 'In that case you will be dismissed,' I answered. 'And why? What have I done to deserve dismissal? I am entitled to know my offence.' 'I have told you,' I said, 'that no offence is charged against you now. If you refuse to obey orders, you will be dismissed, but for disobedience.' He did refuse, and he was dismissed for disobedience.

Some weeks later – I forget how many – he was arrested on the double charge of having in his possession a quantity of dynamite, presumably for unlawful purposes, and a large amount of violently seditious literature. He was arrested in bed, the dynamite and the pamphlets were in his bedroom. He was brought to trial first on the charge of possessing dynamite, and was defended by Tim Healy, afterwards Governor General. Healy pressed with great ingenuity the point that no evidence existed to show what Hegarty meant to do with the dynamite, and so impressed the jury that they acquitted him. As he left the Court, the Crown arrested him on the seditious literature charge. Again he was defended by Healy, who this time induced the jury to disagree. A third trial followed, with the same counsel, and on that occasion Healy, or some other power, was even more successful, for Hegarty was acquitted, and the prosecutions ended. The next morning, as I was walking down to my Office, I met Sir Neville Chamberlain walking up towards the Castle. I stopped him, and said, 'Have you heard that Hegarty is acquitted?' 'No, how did that happen', he said, 'I thought the evidence so clear.' 'It was,' I said, 'but the point is this, – not the diabolical cleverness of Healy, but the fact that the acquittal was by a mixed jury, five Protestants, I believe, and seven Catholics.' 'It is odd that a mixed jury should acquit,' he said; 'they were more likely to disagree. 'Yes,' I answered, 'One would say that in agreeing to acquit they must have been under the influence of some strong motive.' 'Such as what?' he asked, though I think he knew well enough. 'Why, only two would be strong enough,' I answered, 'bribery and fear.' 'Fear, then,' answered Chamberlain, dropping his voice, 'but of what?' 'The I.R.B.' I answered, and we went each his way. This was the first occasion on which, at this fresh crisis of Irish affairs, I had cause to suspect the use of terror as a political resource. But of course terror was no new thing in Ireland.

It would have been hard to miss the significance of cases such as these, even if the public risks which they suggested

103

had not been present to my mind already. My difficulty was how to form an idea of the extent to which my large staff had yielded to disloyalty. To show alarm, or doubt, seemed likely to increase the mischief. Intentional treachery is rare. Most men and women are honest to their duty, once undertaken. But some were not. How was I to discover them? Police and Army reports gave me my only basis of fact, and even those had to be used with caution, since they were often uncertain in tone and judgment, so that they supplied rather starting points for enquiry than definite conclusions, and to take their implications as proved would have been unjust. Army Intelligence was shrewd, as I have shown, but not immune from hasty suspicion. I felt my duty was double, – first to secure the public interest, but next, and not less, to protect my staff from punishment due to unjust suspicion. To strike at the guilty, and strike hard, was the one chance of holding my staff steady. To strike at the loyal in error would be fatal. But who was loyal, and who disloyal? It was vital to know.

I took the Police and Army reports, and classified them in three groups, labelling the first 'Dangerous', the second 'Potentially dangerous,' the third 'Probably negligible.' The first group was small, at no time containing more than a dozen names. These were selected from the reports, and comprised all members of the staff whom I found to be in more than casual communication with the small group of men in Dublin whom I knew to be dangerous plotters. These men were known in Dublin to all who cared to know of them, and I may say that all were shot after the rebellion among the group of sixteen rebels for whom there was no pardon. This fact shows that my principle of classification was not wrong, for men in frequent intercourse with rebels must be presumed to be in sympathy with them. But, granting the soundness of the principle, I was still far from being able to purge the Irish Post Office, for I had still to convince my chief and colleagues in London that there was danger in the situation, and this they refused resolutely to admit, telling me

I had let myself be frightened by heady police officers and soldiers, and that no movement in Ireland need cause a moment's anxiety. Strong Unionists were as contemptuous as Liberals. All alike scouted the idea that Ireland could give serious trouble, and in this view my apprehensions and suggestions broke idly and spent themselves in vain.

My problem, in fact, was, as I said, no problem at all in the eyes of those at St Martin's le Grand, who naturally accepted Mr Birrell's optimism, and as there was no problem, it followed that no instructions were needed for my guidance. I saw this well enough. But it seemed right to make an effort to discover whether what I was doing was all that could be done, and accordingly I made a full copy of my classified list of suspects in the Post Office, and attached a covering memorandum setting forth the principles on which I framed it, and explaining in each case what I had done, and what discussions I had held with the Under Secretary, so as to assure myself that in all matters of importance the Irish Government and the Post Office were not at variance. I sent this up with a personal note asking whether it was regarded as a complete discharge of my duty in unfamiliar circumstances. No reply whatever reached me. I waited three months, during which the tension in Ireland increased, and then wrote again, asking once more to be told whether my action was approved, or whether there was anything else that I could do. This time a note from the Private Secretary reached me, saying the matter was under consideration, and I should hear further. But neither at that time, some three months before the rebellion, nor at any subsequent period, was I told whether I was right or wrong, and still less was any other course of action suggested to me. Nor, to this day, do I know what the Postmaster General thought, if he thought at all.

I do not think however that my labour was wasted. For the time was to come in which the reputation of the Post Office would have been deeply prejudiced, had I proved unable to clear it of the reproach of negligence in a vital matter. Even at the moment, and unable as I was to see what was approaching, I felt the advantage of having clarified my ideas by thorough study of the facts available to me. I was conscious of having done my best, and though I often wished for a confidant, I saw none, even in my own office, whom I could confide in. My second in command, James MacMahon, was deeply involved in Nationalist politics, the intimate friend of many Irish members, and in close relations with the Roman Catholic bishops. Priests, in fact, haunted his office, and I could not but feel that it was not to him that I ought to confide my anxieties at that critical time, when it was not safe to trust men freely. There were sound men among his subordinates, but I could not go past him to consult them, and so I kept my counsel. I do not now think that I was wrong.

Hampered as I was by indifference in London, I set myself steadily to use every occasion which presented itself of perfecting my list of suspects, and proceeding against any of those included in the dangerous class whose actions gave me the material. Cautious as they were, I got it sometimes. But hardly ever could I convince the Postmaster General of the desirability of action. In my memory there rises up the case of Cornelius Collins, a clerk in the Accountant's Office, known to be of extreme and dangerous views, but so clever that his tracks were always covered. At last the police reports gave me evidence not only that he was in frequent communication with men afterwards shot as rebel leaders, but that he had been present at a highly seditious meeting held in the south. One must remember that this was wartime, when sedition and treason are not far apart. I knew also that Collins was drawing into his net one after another of his colleagues who, but for him, would have run straight. The man in fact was dangerous, and I recommended that he be sent to London in an equivalent position, – a light recommendation, of which, on looking back, I scarcely approved. Probably I thought at the time that it would be useless to suggest sharper courses, and indeed I had always to remember that my one chance of getting anything done was to be studiously moderate.

Light as the discipline was, however, it was too heavy for the Postmaster General, who instructed me to warn Collins personally of the effect on his career of continuing his association with disloyal organisations. I did so, and Collins at once began to fence with me. 'What are these associations?' he asked indignantly. 'I specify none, I answered, 'I warn you in terms which are quite general, and it is for you to interpret them, remembering that the warning is meant seriously, and that this is wartime.' 'But evidently,' he insisted, 'you mean that I must drop my connexion with the Gaelic Athletic Association. May I not take interest in Irish sport.' 'I did not mention the Gaelic Athletic Association,' I replied, 'I warned you in general terms.' 'But you meant that?' he went on. 'I do not intend to be more explicit,' I replied. He continued to press me, but with no result. This was a few weeks before the rebellion broke out. When it did, one of the first persons arrested was Cornelius Collins, who was caught in Kerry, endeavouring to join Sir Roger Casement, and who had in his possession incriminating papers relating to the Irish Republican Brotherhood. Evidently, he was near the heart of the movement. My recommendation that he be removed from Ireland erred in leniency, if at all, and the refusal to accept it was a grave error.

It was rather fortunate that I had by this time gained the trust and confidence of large sections of my staff, who had convinced themselves of my intention to be just. They had warrant for this, but that story would be too long to tell. I did not, even at this time of suspicion, lose their confidence and a conspicuous proof of it was given, when a deputation of the staff at Cork asked to see me, and laid before me, temperately and quietly, the fears under which they worked when they saw Army suspicions falling first on one and then on another, so that no man's career was safe. I heard them out, and saw in them sincerity. I thought them honest. Accordingly, I told them that I sat there to distinguish just from unjust suspicion. That from the latter I would protect them to the utmost of my power, and that I felt sure of support from the Postmaster General. But, I added none among them who gave cause for just suspicion or failed in loyalty, or associated with seditious persons, would have help or protection from me. I told them there was but one line of safety, to be loyal and honest in their duty. So long as they were, but so long only, I was on their side. They thanked me, and went away.

It is difficult to recall the stages of the deepening conviction of those days that some outbreak was impending. The greater anxieties of the war deadened our minds even then. It even seemed to matter little, when the greater hazard was at stake. I remember that Lord Granard wrote to me from Gallipoli, asking for my opinion as to what was coming in Ireland, and I replied that barricades were coming, and that I thought we should see grape shot in the streets of Dublin ere long. I remember, too, that two days before the outbreak my son Nevil came into my room at the Post Office, saying he did not like the look of things in Dublin, and would be happier about me if I were armed. Accordingly, he induced me to take from my safe the Colt Automatic which my son Fred used in the few weeks of splendid service which preceded his mortal wound near Armentières. He cleaned it, charged the magazine and four other clips, and laid the whole in a short drawer of my desk, saying 'Now you have thirty shots, and I feel happier about you.' And there the automatic lay on the morning of Easter Monday. I wonder often what I should have done with it, had I been still in my office when the rebels rushed it, instead of missing that crisis by something less than half an hour.

There was no great tension in the air during that week end in Dublin. I was aware personally of some anxiety, for Sir Matthew Nathan told me on the Saturday at the Castle that a prisoner of consequence had been taken in Kerry, and that some risk existed of an attempt at rescue as he was brought through Dublin on his way to London. He did not mention a name, nor did I ask, though I surmised that it must be Sir Roger Casement. Sir Matthew hinted at military precautions in the south, and possible restrictions on the use of postal services by the public. But said nothing of any outbreak in Dublin, nor can I think he had in his mind any serious apprehension of what occurred. If he had, more precautions would certainly have been taken; nor can I think that being in confidential talk with me, he would have omitted such a word of warning as would have put me on my guard, and given me a chance of protecting the Post Office, not to mention the private property which he knew me to have stored there when I gave up my house, after Fred's death, when the associations of it became too keenly painful. But we parted without hint of danger, and for me the Sunday passed quietly.

That night, Sunday, a dance was given by the Gaelic Athletic Association, largely attended by those classes from which the rebellion derived its strength. The dance stood in some close relation to the outbreak. Many of those present were in the secret, and I know of a servant girl, who being faithful, like many of her class, to her master, and even more to her master's children, woke her young mistress early on the Monday morning, and begged her earnestly to stay within doors, since something terrible was about to happen. If, however, some few were warned, they were few indeed. The city bore its usual aspect that Monday morning as I went down after breakfast to the Sackville Street club, where I read the papers, and then went into my office, a few houses away, intending to write letters, and remain till lunch. I was still in the midst of my first letter, when my telephone rang, and Sir Matthew Nathan spoke, asking me to go up to the Castle. He gave no reason, but I surmised some need for such steps as he had suggested two days before. I locked my desk, gave the key of my room to the porter, who was the only person on duty, the day being a bank holiday, and left, saying I should be back in half an hour. I never saw my room again till the whole building was gutted and burnt to a shell.

I saw nothing unusual as I walked up to the Castle. Nathan had with him Major Price, the Army Intelligence Officer. He turned to me as I came in, and told me there was serious trouble in Kerry, where a ship had been seized with German Officers on board, and material for a rising. Casement, however, whom he then named, had been conveyed to London under guard, with no attempt at rescue. The position was serious, and he desired, me to take immediate steps for denying the use of the Telephone and Telegraph service over large areas of Southern Ireland to all but military and Naval use. I said that was too important a matter to be settled verbally, and I must have it in writing. 'Very well,' he said, 'You write out what you want, and I will sign it.' I was just finishing the necessary order, when a volley of musketry crashed out beneath the window. I looked up. 'What's that?' I asked. 'Oh, that's probably the long promised attack on the Castle,' cried Nathan, jumping up, and leaving the room, while Major Price shouted from the window to some person below, after which he too ran off. I waited for a few minutes, and then went downstairs in search of some explanation. At the foot of the staircase I found all the messengers huddled together in a frightened crowd. They had just seen the policeman at the gate shot through the heart. They were badly shaken.

They had however got the gate of the Upper Castle yard shut. The gate of the lower yard also had been shut. No attack was proceeding, and I found Nathan with the Store keeper breaking open the armoury in the hope of arming the handful of constables of the Dublin Metropolitan Police who formed the only guard of the Castle. He found some revolvers, but no cartridges; so that the constables remained of little use, while the rebels, declaring themselves without opposition ranged at

will about the city, seizing one important building after
another, and posting their proclamation of the Irish Republic
wherever they would. In the handsome building of the
General Post Office, which I had left so short a while before,
the Union Jack was hauled down, and the green flag of the
Irish Republic floated in its place. The Office in fact was
rushed twenty minutes after I had left it, my room being
appropriated for the rebel headquarters. The guard of
soldiers at the door of the Instrument room did their best, but
for some military reason, which I never heard, they had been
deprived of ammunition, without my knowledge. Their rifles
being empty, they retreated inside and barricaded the door.
But the rebels fired through it, shot the sergeant in the face,
and, the post being untenable, the men surrendered. Had I
not been rung up by the Under Secretary, I should have been
the only man armed upon the premises. What then should I
have done? I presume I ought to have tried to hold the
staircase, and keep the mob down. I hope I should have done
so. The certain result would have been that I should have
been shot at once, and the probable result would have been
that the Government in London would have declared the
whole trouble to have arisen from my wicked folly in firing
upon a body of peaceful, if armed, citizens. So much one sees
clearly, for politicians in a difficulty are never fair, and still
less generous. But all else is dark.

Sir Matthew Nathan had no intention of extricating me
from an approaching danger, in the existence of which he did
not in fact believe. He had formed the habit, possibly on
instructions from Mr Birrell, of consulting John Dillon upon
every step he took, and viewing everything through the eyes
of that old and inveterate rebel. Under this fatal influence,
and on the accepted policy of avoiding all measures which
might be provocative, he had omitted all precautions, making
no arrests, and leaving the city during that critical week end
denuded so far of troops that when the Castle gates were shut
on himself, the Attorney General (afterwards Sir James

O'Connor[5]) and me, there was no force nearer than the Curragh which could be used to restore us to freedom. The rebels had posted snipers in the upper windows of houses commanding the exits from the Castle, and were firing on all who left it. It was perhaps worth while for one who had led a very sheltered life to become suddenly one of a besieged garrison, and I do not know that the disquiet of the situation was much relieved by the fact that no attack developed, and that the sounds of fighting were still distant. I remember drawing Nathan's attention to the fact that the small courtyard up and down which he was pacing was commanded by the windows of houses accessible from the street, and could not be considered safe. He agreed, but replied that there were no soldiers to occupy those houses, so that we must take our chance. Why the Castle was not attacked I do not know. The afternoon wore on, and at dusk a battalion of the South Staffords marched in, having come up by train from the Curragh, and lost seven men – so we were told – on the way from Kingsbridge to the Castle. Besieged we may not have been, in a true sense; but the relief with which we watched the cheerful smiles of officers and men as they stacked their arms in the lower courtyard was considerable, for it is clear enough that the rebels could have made us prisoners without loss, and the lot of prisoners during the rebellion was not always comfortable or even safe.

Safe as we felt, in the presence of our own troops, there was enough in the streets of Dublin that night of wild passion and fierce hope to convince the most careless of us that the country stood on the edge of some abyss, and as dark fell the thought recurred oftener than one wished that this sudden outbreak was formidable, and might be timed to coincide with some German stroke, possibly an invasion, – for if that was in fact impossible we had no assurance of it then. When it grew quite dark, the troops attacked the City Hall, at the gate of the Upper Castle yard, which the rebels had occupied, and barricaded. I stood in the lower yard with the Attorney

General, listening to the noise of fighting. The rifle volleys came in crashes, mingled with the tapping of machine guns, and the shattering burst of bombs, so near that they seemed close beside us. The yard was lit by torches, and crowded with men and soldiers, among whom from time to time a woman was carried in, caught in the act of carrying ammunition to the rebels, and fighting like trapped cats. It was a strange and awful scene. I turned to the Attorney General, and said, 'This seems to be the death knell of Home Rule.' Now he was a sane and moderate Nationalist. But he said thoughtfully, 'Upon my soul, I don't know are we fit for it after all.' And then, after a little interval, 'The man I am sorry for is John Redmond.'

It was late before the noise of fighting died away, and not till after midnight did I prevail on the soldiers at the Castle gate to open it sufficiently to let me slip out, and whisk round into a side lane, expecting to get a sniper's bullet between my shoulders as I ran. But nothing happened, and I got back safely to the Royal Hibernian Hotel in Dawson street, where my wife waited for me in considerable anxiety. She has herself told the story of that day in the admirable letters published in a separate volume, and I shall try not to repeat what she says but only to supplement it. She was invaluable to me in the days which followed, and it is not too much to say that throughout the week of active fighting she and I, with one of my Principal clerks who, at great risk, managed to reach me day by day, – I refer to my friend Mr J. J. Coonan, – constituted the General Post Office, for with very few exceptions the staff were unable to pass the cordons of rebels and of soldiers, and we saw nothing of them. One conspicuous officer, Mr Gomersall, the Superintending Engineer, rendered admirable and very plucky service. For the rebels having cut the Telegraph and Telephone wires, with the intention of isolating Dublin from the rest of Ireland, and so from England, the Engineer took a car and drove round the outskirts of the city, picking up the ends of the

113

cables, and leading them in to private circuits which he commandeered for the purpose; and this he did with such success that our communications were kept open throughout the rebellion.

It is perhaps worth while to record, since I have referred to the Irish Republican Brotherhood, to say that while I was sitting with Sir Matthew Nathan during the afternoon of this first day of the rebellion, a constable brought in one of the placards which the rebels were posting as they seized one after another important buildings in the city. It is this placard, or proclamation, from which I quote on Page [101-2] of the present notes, and Sir Matthew passed it across the table for me to see. I had in mind the latest report sent to me from the Intelligence Dept in the Castle, by Nathan's orders, and especially the assertion in this report that the I.R.B. was probably dormant, and might be regarded as negligible. I put my finger on the paragraph which I have quoted, and passed it back to Sir Matthew, with the remark, 'It seems that the I.R.B. is not so dormant after all.' Sir Matthew smiled uncomfortably, but said nothing.

His manner and actions were those of a man who was not cool and steady, but rather bewildered. Nor is this surprising, for it was, and is, manifest that he, as permanent head of the Irish service, and Responsible adviser of Mr Birrell, the Chief Secretary, who as I have said visited Dublin rarely, must bear the blame for neglecting to suppress dangerous associations, and for giving his confidence to those who did not deserve it, such as John Dillon, with whom he used to discuss many matters of consequence, and who dined with him at regular intervals. I think his intercourse with Dillon may have been imposed on him by Mr Birrell, and if so, it is improbable that Sir Matthew would have exercised his own judgment on the point at all, for that would have run counter to his conception of loyalty, expounded more than once by him to me, – a conception differing vitally from that traditional in the Civil Service, which enjoins that the political Head should always know what his chief advisers think. 'What I want from you,' said Lord Buxton to me, as Postmaster General, 'is to give me your best opinion. I may reject it, but I always want to know it.' He was right. But Sir Matthew's view was that his duty lay in finding out what his Chief wished to do, and in helping him to do it without discussion. Any degree of contention, or discussion even, was in his opinion disloyalty.

I dwell on this since it throws light on the events of the previous day, I mean the Sunday before the outbreak, when there was still a last chance of preserving peace. My information was derived from Lord Wimborne, who had replaced Lord Aberdeen as Lord Lieutenant, and with whom my wife and I were lunching at the Vice-regal Lodge a few weeks after the Rebellion. There was, it seems, a Council on that day at the Lodge, and during the discussion Lord Wimborne urged strongly the immediate arrest of the well known dangerous persons who were the mainsprings of the rebellious movement, and most of whom, if not all, were subsequently shot. But Lord Wimborne was not in the Cabinet, and Mr Birrell, who was, but was in London, had empowered Sir Matthew, as his representative, to oppose the Lord Lieutenant, following out to the last the fatal doctrine that nothing must be done which could possibly create friction. The Cabinet authority prevailed, – one wonders whether the voice behind was not John Dillon's. Lord Wimborne, who spoke to me about it with indignation, did not press his view, though I still think that he, as representative of the King, might have brought into play reserve powers, and compelled the arrests. He was not strong enough to do that, and there were no arrests. The consequence that a new and deadly risk was added to the dangers in which England stood, at that grave moment of the war.

If, then, Sir Matthew, whose action had prevented the arrest of ring leaders while there was still time, was shaken and bewildered at the moment of the outbreak, it is little wonder. His reputation was gone. His counsellor had betrayed him. The things he did not believe in were before him. He had failed to guard England from added danger. I do him the justice of believing the perception to have been very bitter to him.

The City Hall, and other important buildings which the rebels had seized, were not recaptured that night. After 10 p.m. the sound of fighting died away; and first the Attorney General (James O'Connor) and then I slipped out of the lower Castle Yard into a lane on the right, and so, through silent streets, I reached the Hibernian Hotel in Dawson Street, where my wife and son were much relieved to see me. Next day, it was obvious at an early hour that to reach the Post Office, on the further side of the river, was impossible; the bridges being held strongly by rebels, while the Post Office itself was known to have been seized a quarter of an hour after I left it, and the green flag of the revolt was flying from its roof. And here I may say that at the outbreak of the war, being uneasy about the risk of a German agent gaining access to the Instrument room, and destroying the Telegraph system by throwing a bomb into the test box, I applied for a guard of soldiers, and such a guard was posted in my presence, the orders being that the sentries were to keep their magazines full, but the cut off close, and were to shoot to stop any unidentified person who approached the Instrument Room. But for some reason, and at some later date, though when or why, I could not discover, in the post-rebellion confusion, the sentinels had been deprived of ammunition, and left at their posts with empty rifles. On the rebel attack, they retreated into the Instrument Room, barricading the door. But the rebels fired through, shooting the Sergeant in the face. There was no alternative but to surrender. The soldiers were helpless, and the blame lies with those, probably civilians, who disarmed them. If I, who had a revolver with thirty shots, had been still in the Office, and had attempted, as I hope I should, to hold the staircase, I should have been shot at once, and what is worse, I should have been blamed by a frightened Government seeking for a scapegoat.

I have said that by the courageous enterprise of Mr Gomersall the adverse effect of the loss of the Telegraph Office was neutralised, the wires being led into Amiens Street, which was, and remained in our hands. The Telephone office, off Dame Street, was also ours. But with those exceptions there was no Post Office, save the room which I had commandeered at the Hibernian Hotel, and the Telephone circuit which I had appropriated. At that Telephone, my wife, or I, sat all day long. Her cool pluck, and excellent good sense, were invaluable to me, and indeed to the public interest.

Shortly after breakfast the next morning the Police rang me up, by direction of the Under Secretary, asking me to go to the Castle. I asked by what route. 'By Dame Street,' was the answer, 'That is quite safe today.' I was surprised, but to Dame Street I went, and was just turning into it, opposite to Trinity College, when a storm of bullets swept down the street, evidently from rebel rifles, and was answered by sharp successive volleys from Trinity College. The police were wrong; and I give this incident to show that even they were quite unable to foretell from hour to hour where the fighting would break out. The bearing of the fact will be seen as I proceed. I reached the Castle by devious back lanes and found, on that as on other mornings, the Sir Matthew Nathan had little to say to me which could not have been said over the telephone, without calling me away from the only point at which I could be of service, or exposing me to the quite real risks of the streets. Indeed, knowing that my only substitute at the telephone was my wife, he summoned me the next day to the Castle four times, at some personal risk, and much interruption, without any reason of real advantage.

It is the less necessary to relate in detail the events of the following eight days because my wife has told them vividly in

117

her published letters. I shall set down merely what supplements her tale. It was difficult to discover what was happening. For instance, I had occasion that morning to see the Engineer, and as he had incurred some risk a few hours before in coming down from Terenure to see me, I thought it unfair to bring him down again, and set out to visit him. I went up Grafton Street to the corner of St Stephen's Green, whence looking up towards Harcourt Street I could see a barricade of upturned motors etc about half way along the Green, near the College of Surgeons. There was a brisk exchange of rifle and machine gun fire going on between the rebels entrenched at the further side of the Green, and our own soldiers in the Shelbourne Hotel; and with this sound ringing through the air, it was difficult to look trustfully on a barricade, though it seemed abandoned. I asked a few people what the position was, and as they were assuring me the fighting at that point was over, I saw a man walk through the barricade towards us. If he could pass, it was clear I could; so I went on and entered Harcourt street, which was the direct and only way to Terenure. I had not gone far however when the whole street was blocked by a crowd of people swept back by soldiers, and finding it impossible to go on, I turned again into Stephen's Green, and walked back the way I came. As I drew near the College of Surgeons, I noticed several windows broken by rifle bullets, and in the same moment a bullet flew past my nose and broke a window on my left. I then saw for the first time that the College of Surgeons was held by rebels, and it was under heavy cross fire from the Shelbourne Hotel. It was in fact the command of that virago the Countess Markiewicz, and I was at that moment crossing the line of fire. This may serve to show the difficulty of ascertaining where one could go in safety; for clearly the information given by those I questioned in Grafton Street was wrong.

I set these two illustrations of the uncertainties in Dublin side by side because they throw a curious light on proposals made to me authoritatively either on that day, or the next. Sir Matthew rang me up and asked me to go down to the Castle. When I arrived he said he wanted to know from me whether I could not restore postal services over at least some part of the area of Dublin. I asked 'What part?' 'That is what I want you to tell me,' he said. 'But how can I?' I asked. 'I have no official information whatever, and no staff, as you are aware. You, on the other hand, as head of the Civil Government of Ireland, have full reports of police, and perhaps of military. Surely, I might ask you to indicate the districts which you think safe enough to justify me in putting postmen in uniform upon the streets.' 'It is useless to ask me that,' he said, 'for that is what I want from you.' 'I must press you,' I said, 'that I have no means whatever of forming a sound opinion. Will you not at least give me the reports you have, and let me study them.' 'No,' he said, 'I want your sole judgment, and I want it in writing by four o'clock.' I protested that this was scarcely fair, but in vain. Finding it was impossible to move Sir Matthew, I returned to my hotel, and had scarcely reached it when the Lord Lieutenant rang me up, and put the same question. Half an hour later the Irish Office in London pressed the same point on me, and it seemed obvious that the Government, being pressed in the House of Commons, wanted to get up and declare that the rising in Dublin had been exaggerated, that some degree of order was restored, and that postal deliveries had been resumed over considerable areas of the City. The fact that the rebels were firing on any one who wore uniform, even the Fire Brigade, and that the postmen would certainly have been shot, was either unknown to them, or treated as of no importance. To me it was the governing consideration. I had no member of my staff to consult with. But the case seemed clear. I rang up the mail cart Contractor, and asked him whether he felt justified in sending out his vans and drivers into any part of Dublin. He said, rather indignantly, 'You must know the answer to that question. Why do you put it to me? 'Because it is pressed on me,' I said. 'May I take it that you will not send out the vans?' 'You may,' he answered. I then wrote at once a short report to the effect that being asked for my opinion as to the practicability of resuming normal postal services over some part of Dublin, and having at my command no official information about the state of the City, I could only say that my own observation led me to the conclusion that no such steps were practicable at the time, and that the lives of postmen would be in great danger if they appeared upon the streets. I therefore declined respectfully to order them to go out.

I took this myself to Sir Matthew Nathan, who received it ungraciously, not concealing his opinion that my attitude was obstructive. I had not, however, nor have I now, the least doubt that I was right.

As I conceived my duty in the difficult and changing circumstances, and in the absence of any guidance whatever from my Chiefs in London, who left me throughout to take my own line, I was bound in reason both to protect the interests of the Crown and public, so far as I could, and also to protect honest members of the Post Office staff against punishment which could not be shown or presumed with probability to be deserved, for they had no other protector. The fair and just discharge of these two functions was not easy. Both however were vitally important, and mistakes were likely to be disastrous. I thought it of the first consequence to act both firmly and justly. How difficult that was may be seen from what happened in the latter days of the rebellion. Sir John Maxwell was then in command, having replaced General Friend. The revolt was broken, and the soldiers were arresting large numbers of men of whom some certainly had been fighting, though their rifles were cast away, while others had been only curious spectators. The crowds were such that discrimination was impossible, and the arrests were wholesale. There were accordingly in my hands long lists of Post Office men, and some women, under arrest, and detained. The problem was to decide which were guilty, for it was clear that none who had fought against the Crown ought to be restored to the service of the Crown, having in fact dismissed themselves. The trouble lay in finding evidence of guilt.

As I was beginning to work at that problem, an officer from Army Headquarters was shown in. 'The General understands,' he said, 'that you are able to indicate certain members of your staff who have taken part in the rebellion.' 'That is not so,' I said, 'I have lists of officers arrested and detained. But their cases must in justice be examined before they can be pronounced guilty, and dismissed; for some among them may probably be innocent.' He agreed that the conditions in the streets were such as to render just distinctions difficult. 'But,' he said, 'if you will give me your list I will tell the General what you say, and you shall be consulted before anything is done.' I gave him the lists, impressing on him clearly that they could not be regarded as anything more than the starting point of an enquiry. The next morning the lists were returned to me, marked in the General's own hand 'Dismiss,' opposite some score of names, or more, but without any indication of evidence justifying the sentences. I did not see my way to dismiss men and women without evidence. The declaration of military law did not seem to justify the abandonment of any effort to distinguish guilt from innocence. I went up to Army Headquarters. The General was absent from Dublin, and the officers I saw could only say that in his absence nothing could be done. 'You mean,' I said, 'that I must at once dismiss these men?' 'Since military law is declared, you must indeed,' was the reply. 'Well, gentlemen,' I said, 'the Post Office does not dismiss men without evidence that it is acting justly. I shall suspend these instructions. But I will go to London tonight, lay the matter before the Postmaster General, whose authority is supreme in his Department, and take his instructions.' It seemed to them unheard of that any one should hesitate to carry out the order of the General. I did as I had said, however, and early the next morning I put the whole case before the Postmaster General, Mr Pease and Sir Evelyn Murray, the Secretary. They approved what I had done and as the result of somewhat protracted negotiations, a small Committee was sent to Dublin, consisting of Sir Guy Fleetwood Wilson,[6] and Sir William Byrne,[7] who investigated the various cases, rather perfunctorily, and assumed the responsibility of indicating who were to be dismissed, – a number, I may add, considerably less than had been indicated by the General. The procedure created at least some protection against injustice.

NOTES

1. A retired Indian civil servant.
2. The King's Own Scottish Borderers.
3. The Royal Commission on the Rebellion in Ireland.
4. Joint Second Secretary of the Post Office, 1914–19.
5. O'Connor, who was knighted in 1925, was at the time of the Rising Solicitor General for Ireland. He was not appointed Attorney General until December 1916.
6. A retired official whose career had spanned both the British and Indian civil services.
7. A barrister with a long record of public service. He was Under-Secretary to the Irish Office, 1916–18.

Index